The Fifth Evangelist

The Fifth Evangelist

A. M. HUNTER

[Archibald Macbride]

SCM PRESS LTD

334 00477 2

First published 1980
by SCM Press Ltd
58 Bloomsbury Street, London WC1

Photoset by Input Typesetting Ltd
and printed in Great Britain by
Richard Clay (The Chaucer Press) Ltd,
Bungay, Suffolk

Contents

Preface

St Paul has often been sadly misunderstood, both by Christians and non-Christians. Part One of this book is a personal – indeed autobiographical – invitation to the reader to think of Paul as 'the fifth evangelist, the first in point of time and of value both'. Then, from his letters, I have portrayed him, in turn, as writer, liberator, pastor, theologian, churchman, friend and saint.

In Part Two, after chapters on St John and 'the new look' that has come over his Gospel in our time, I have added further essays on the Lord's supper, the Holy Spirit, prayer, preaching and the church's hymns. The final chapters concentrate on those three little words, faith, love and hope, which, properly understood, take us back to the Church's first beginnings, as still today they sum up what it means to be a Christian.

Scriptural quotations are mostly from the RSV and the NEB.

Once again I am deeply indebted for help, both with the manuscript and the proofs, to my friend and neighbour the Revd David G. Gray B.D., formerly minister of St Peter's Church, Dundee.

A. M. HUNTER

Ayr
January 1980

1

The Fifth Evangelist

'The ugly little Jew who was the cause of the chief defects in Christian theology' – thus, in the nineteenth century, Ernest Renan (who cared more for beauty than for truth) dismissed St Paul. In 1905, while the liberal theologians still possessed the field, and Paul was commonly regarded as the arch-sophisticator of the Gospel, P. T. Forsyth took a very different view. 'I call Paul the Fifth Evangelist', he told the Congregational Union of England and Wales, 'and we ought to call him the first in point of time and of value both.'[1] Thirteen years later, Karl Barth's commentary on *Romans* fell like a bombshell into the theologians' camp and, behold, he was on the side of Forsyth. Paul, he wrote in his Preface, 'as a child of his time addressed his contemporaries. As prophet and apostle of the Kingdom of God, he veritably speaks to all men of every age.' No wonder men were later to call Forsyth 'a Barthian before Barth'. For both believed that our deepest spiritual problems are, basically, the problems of Paul, and declared that, if we are enlightened by the brightness of Paul's answers, those answers must be ours too.

Confession, they say, is good for the soul. And if I start autobiographically, it is not because the story of my spiritual pilgrimage is important or unique – it is neither – but because, starting like Forsyth as a liberal, I have come to the same conclusion as he did.

When I began my New Testament study, the gospel meant for me (as for the great liberal Harnack) the Fatherhood of God, the

1

law of love, and the infinite value of the human soul, with Jesus as the supreme proclaimer of these sovereign truths. My christology might have been summed up as 'Jesus, divinest when thou most art man'. My puzzle was Paul. I had no convincing answer to the charge that Paul was the great perverter of the gospel. At the same time I was haunted by the suspicion, later to be confirmed by T. W. Manson,[2] that somehow 'the liberals had failed to interpret the New Testament as the Word of God.'

Then, in 1935, to me as a young minister in Perthshire, came light from an unexpected quarter. For a week I played host to one of Germany's greatest (though unduly sceptical) New Testament scholars, under whom I had previously studied, Bultmann of Marburg. When I asked him if he could suggest a theme for my own research, he replied, 'Why, the dependence of St Paul on his Christian predecessors. Try to appraise Paul's debt to those who were Christians before him.' And Bultmann recommended some books for my reading.

The result, published in 1940 as *Paul and His Predecessors*, was to convince me of two things. First, Paul was no Christian Columbus voyaging through strange seas alone in the first century. He was but one, though the greatest, of many who in three decades carried the good news from Jerusalem to Rome.

Second, though Paul's theology bears clear marks of his own profound Christian experience, the gospel which he preached was, as he himself avows in I Cor. 15.11, the same as that preached by the other apostles. To be sure, Paul had a creative and original mind; but the thing about which he writes is not his own discovery: it is the common tradition of the Christian faith which he had himself 'received' from those who were Christians before him.

What, then, were Paul's debts to these men?
1. The *kerygma*, or preached Gospel, as in I Cor. 15.3ff.
2. The confession of Jesus as Saviour and Lord (e.g. Rom. 10.9).
3. The Holy Spirit as the divine dynamic of the new life.
4. The conception of the church as the new people of God.
5. The triad, faith, love, hope.
6. Various 'words of the Lord' (e.g. I Cor. 7.10; 9.14).

7. The sacraments of baptism and the Lord's supper.

8. Some early Christian hymns (e.g. Phil. 2.6–11).

9. The hope of Christ's coming in glory (1 Cor. 16.22).

10. Not a little (when you remember that we are dealing with epistles, not gospels) about 'the Jesus of history'. Born of David's line (Rom. 1.3), Jesus had brothers, one called James (I Cor. 9.5; Gal. 1.19). On earth his lot was that of a poor man (II Cor. 8.9). In character, he was 'gentle and magnanimous' (II Cor. 10.1; cf. Matt. 11.29). Patient under trials (II Thess. 3.5), he was ever obedient to God's will (Rom. 5.19; Phil. 2.8). His ministry was exercised among the Jews (Rom. 15.8), and he had twelve apostles (I Cor. 15.5), two of them named Peter and John (Gal. 2.9). Before the Jews killed him (I Thess. 2.15) – indeed 'on the night he was betrayed' – he instituted the Lord's supper (I Cor. 11.23ff.). He was crucified and buried. On the third day, God raised him from the dead, designating him his Son 'with power' (Rom. 1.4). Thereafter he appeared alive to all the apostles and many witnesses (I Cor. 15.5–7).

All in all, a pretty deep indebtedness, and more than enough to acquit Paul of the charge of being the great corrupter of the gospel!

This, however, was only a beginning. The liberals had commonly referred to Paul as 'the second founder of Christianity'. The falsity of this view became evident as I now discovered the true relation between Jesus and Paul. Of two mistakes they had been guilty. First, they had tried to tell the story of Jesus without a christology. (It was Schweitzer, who, besides demolishing the liberal portrait of Jesus, taught us that this cannot be done. Hoskyns and Davey went further.[3] 'The riddle of the New Testament,' they said, 'is really a christological one. It is Jesus Christ himself.')

The liberals' second error had been to compare two quite incomparable persons, Jesus in his own historical situation, and Paul in his. Rightly understood, the theology of Paul (and of his Christian predecessors) is faith's answer to the saving work of God in Christ. In the four gospels Christ is the pilgrim Son of God who, to ransom the many from their sins (Mark 10.45),

3

travels the road appointed for him by his Father, and at last dies an accursed death for them on the cross. *Per contra*, the first apostles and Paul, in the light of the resurrection and the day of Pentecost, look back on Christ's finished work (John 19.30) and the salvation which it has brought. That is to say, the gospel *about* Christ has replaced the good news of God's inbreaking rule which Jesus had proclaimed and himself embodied, because, by the resurrection and the Pentecostal event, Jesus has become all that the kingdom contained. 'The Gospel of the Kingdom,' as Forsyth put it, 'was Christ in essence; the risen Christ was the Kingdom come with power' (cf. Mark 9.1 with Rom. 1.4). He was the truth of his own greatest Gospel.'[4] In short, if we allow for the difference made by the first Easter day and Pentecost, the gospel preached by Paul and his predecessors was not the distortion of the gospel Jesus proclaimed but its fulfilment.

Not yet, however, was my quest at an end. Further study of the teaching of Christ and of Paul showed that at point after point the Lord and his apostle were at one.

For both Jesus and Paul the Law is the revelation of God's will for men, as both lay the emphasis on its *moral* demands and find its kernel in the law of love, or *agapé*.[5]

Both Jesus and Paul teach justification by faith, Paul in his own forensic categories, Jesus in his own moving human terms. Reduced to its simplest form, justification (acquittal by God) is his free forgiveness for the penitent sinner; and Christ's supreme parable about the Father and his scapegrace son is a perfect picture of it. Again, in his story about the Pharisee and the publican (Luke 18.9–14) we find not only the doctrine but Paul's very word for it (*dedikaiōmenos*: 'acquitted'). Even Christ's promise to the penitent thief (Luke 23.43) is best taken as an example of the same thing. But we are not yet at the end of the evidence for the point being made.

At first sight, the Sermon on the Mount (Matt. 5–7) and Paul's Epistle to the Romans seem poles apart. But are they? Paul begins his letter with the sin of man (Rom. 1.18–3.20) for which the grace of God in Christ is the remedy (Rom. 3.21–8.39). Jesus

4

opens his sermon with, 'How blest are those who know their need of God!' (Matt. 5.3 NEB); and though he does not speak of sin as Paul does, he assumes man's fallen state (Matt. 7.11, 'If you, then, being evil, etc.'), and makes it clear how far, in Paul's phrase,' we 'fall short of the glory of God', i.e. the divine likeness man was meant to bear (Rom. 3.23). 'There is no account of sin,' it has been said, 'to match the Sermon'. Who is sufficient for the towering moral demands he makes in it? What mortal man is able to fulfil them completely? Not Tolstoy or any other! If the Sermon teaches us how God means us men to live – 'You must be perfect as your heavenly Father is perfect' – God have mercy on us all, sinners that we are!

It is wrong, therefore, to say that Paul preached a different gospel from that which Christ proclaimed. The same saving act of God is the theme of both gospels and epistles. But, whereas Jesus, in his passion sayings, speaks of the act on *this* side of Calvary, Paul and his predecessors describe it from the vantage-point of Easter and Pentecost. On their essential views of sin and salvation, Jesus and Paul are at one. Yet one decisive difference there is between them, and none realized it better than Paul. Jesus knew himself to be the Christ (or Messiah) of God and his only Son. Paul is the servant and envoy of this Christ. He is the apostle: Jesus is his Lord, and his the only name given under heaven whereby men may be saved.

Now let us examine more closely what Forsyth meant when he styled Paul the fifth evangelist.

Here the question which arises is: Was Christ a part of the Gospel he proclaimed? The apostles and Paul answered 'Yes'; the liberals said 'No'.

Suppose we appeal to the synoptic gospels for an answer. (The liberals discounted the witness of the Fourth Gospel; wrongly, as 'the new look on John's Gospel' now shows.) Do the first three gospels yield us no more than a supreme prophet of the Father-hood of God, a figure with no central place in the good news he proclaimed? On the contrary, they show us one who knows himself to be the fulfiller of God's revelation to his ancient people

Israel (Matt. 5.17), one who solemnly affirms that on men's acceptance or rejection of himself hangs their eternal destiny (Matt. 10.32; Luke 9.26), one whose claim to be central to his own gospel and the sole mediator of the saving knowledge of God the holy Father comes to supreme expression in his great thanksgiving:

All things have been delivered to me by my Father,
And no one knows the Son except the Father,
And no one knows the Father except the Son,
And anyone to whom the Son chooses to reveal him.

(Matt. 11.27f.)

(On this point none did more than Denney in his *Jesus and the Gospel* to show, by a study of Jesus' sayings, in Mark and 'Q', that they reveal a person 'who is not only equal to the place which Christian faith assigns him but who assumed that place naturally and spontaneously as his own'.)

Yet this is but half of the truth. The great thing which Jesus brought to the world was not a doctrine but a *deed* – the deed of the cross in which his ministry found its fulfilment and completion. 'Now is the judgment of this world', St John records him as saying, 'now shall the prince of this world be cast out' (John 12.31); and again, 'I, if I be lifted up, will draw all men unto me' (12.32). The claim of the crucified Christ is greater (Forsyth says) than any explicit in his mouth during his ministry. We cannot therefore allow the liberals (or such of them as survive today) to repudiate the New Testament account of Christ for one of their own nineteenth-century making. They have no right to say that, in order to find Christ's Christianity, we must confine ourselves to certain selected words of his from the synoptic gospels. As Denney said somewhere, and truly, 'It needs the whole of the New Testament to show who Christ is.'

Let us therefore now consider *the apostles' testimony to Christ in their epistles*.

Is theirs a true interpretation of Christ and his work? All turns on the place we assign them in the economy of revelation. Granted that God revealed himself in Christ, is the apostles'

6

account of it just man construing, so that their testimony is no more authoritative than the reflections or speculations of later Christians?

Let us (says Forsyth) distinguish between the material and the formal revelation. In the material sense Christ was the final revelation of God (cf. Heb. 1.1f.). In him God spoke and acted: in Christ God was his own apostle.

Yet this revelation was not complete until it was formally consummated in the interpretation. As a lesson is not finally taught until it is learnt, so Christ's work was not finished until its meaning was got home. Therefore when men ask, Why did not Christ explain himself and his saving purpose more fully? The answer is that he did – *after his earthly work was done*. But where? In the apostolic writings of men like Paul, Peter and John, and by the Holy Spirit.

Was not this what Christ himself had promised when, in the upper room, he spoke of the Holy Spirit guiding his apostles into all the truth? 'He (the Spirit) will take what is mine and declare it unto you' (John 16.12–15). Only after the coming of the Spirit would they fully understand his work and words.

This is Paul's theme in I Cor. 2, a classic chapter for the psychology of apostolic inspiration, and his conclusion is: 'We (the apostles) possess the mind of Christ' (I Cor. 2.16 NEB). This means: 'We have the spiritual intention – the theology – of Christ.' 'Our thoughts are Christ's thoughts', is how Moffatt renders it.

Now we may perceive the apostles' true place in the economy of revelation. We are not in the same position as they. They were unique. Their uniqueness does not consist merely in their historical situation, though we must allow due weight to the fact that they were 'eye-witnesses of his majesty' (II Peter 1.16; cf. I John 1.1–4). What did they see? Not mere events, but a person whose self-manifestation they accepted by faith. And what they give us is not primarily their own reactions but what, through the Holy Spirit, they received from the living Christ, i.e. revelation.

The apostlic letters, therefore, are not the intuitions of religious geniuses. The testimony they contain is the authentic teaching of the living Christ given them through the Holy Spirit. For 'the presence of the Spirit is Christ's own presence in spirit'. In short, to sum up in Forsyth's own words: 'The apostolic documents are the prolongation of the message of Jesus. They are Christ himself interpreting his finished work through men in whom not they lived but Christ in them. Christ in the apostles interpreted his finished work as truly as in his lifetime he interpreted his unfinished work.'[6]

A high doctrine of apostolic inspiration indeed! But is it not the true one? And does it not explain why Forsyth called Paul 'the fifth evangelist', describing him as 'first in point of time and of value both'?

Nearly nineteen centuries separate Forsyth from Paul. Yet, as you study the men and their Christian thinking, you discover how much the two have in common.

Both underwent a decisive conversion experience. Of Paul's we know from his letters and the book of Acts. Forsyth tells us less about his, but of its effect he says: 'I was turned from a lover of love to an object of grace.' And henceforth Paul's great word 'grace' – the unmerited love of God in Christ to sinners – pervades all his writings, as in the eighteenth century it had done John Newton's.[7] On the levity of liberalism he had turned his back. Now the burden of his gospel was to be God the holy Father, the living Christ, and the power of the cross by which God had in principle redeemed men from their sin and guilt.

Again, the theologies of both Paul and Forsyth were hammered out not in academic cloisters but in the hurly-burly of busy ministries – Paul's in great cities of the Roman empire like Antioch and Corinth. Forsyth's in huge industrial cities of England like Manchester and London. If Paul was a Christian prophet interpreting salvation in Christ to the hard pagan world of the first century AD, Forsyth was a like prophet for the twentieth century, proclaiming the grace and judgment of God to a British public that was not bothering about its sins, in the years that led up to the horrors of the First World War. (See chapter

8

I of Forsyth's *The Justification of God*.) If Paul in his day had spoken of 'the wrath of God being revealed from heaven against the ungodliness and wickedness of men' (Rom. 1.18), no less trenchantly did Forsyth indict the sinfulness of his own generation and point to the War as God's *nemesis* upon it. (Yet Forsyth also said, in a much-quoted word: 'If God cares enough to be angry, he cares enough to redeem.' To this Paul would have said 'Amen'.)

Yet it is when you compare Forsyth's theology as a whole with Paul's that you perceive how alike the two men were in their thinking.[8]

With Paul, Forsyth holds fast the dogma of 'original sin', 'the corruption of man's heart' (as Browning called it), a universal malady which has infected not the individual only but the whole race. How it first came into the world he does not speculate. There it is now as a stark, ineluctable reality and curse. Sin expressing itself in guilt is the evil with which God in Christ came to deal. For the essence of sin is revolt against a holy God; 'we men are not just silly sheep gone astray: we are rebels taken with weapons in our hands.'

For both Paul and Forsyth, revelation *is* redemption – God in Christ coming and acting for our salvation. And the seat of this revelation is to be found not in the heart but in the cross. *Per crucem ad lucem!* 'Through the cross to light!' There, at Calvary, we see God in his Son Jesus Christ taking the burden of the world's sin on himself and, in principle, redeeming a whole human race.

Forsyth's teaching about the cross reminds us both of St Paul's and of MacLeod Campbell's (in his *The Nature of the Atonement*). Christ on his cross is God himself saving in his own way. On that cross, as our representative, Christ confessed God's holiness, and the satisfaction he offered to God on sinners' behalf was one of perfect obedience to his Father's will. Thus, by the atonement (which, on the third day, God sealed and crowned by the resurrection), Christ won a moral victory over the sinful world which still today, by the Spirit's work, has power to evoke in

9

sinners the response of saving faith and so help to create a new humanity.

Concerning such faith Paul and Forsyth speak with one voice. For Paul, faith which is opposed to works (i.e. the attempt to earn one's salvation by laying up a credit balance of good deeds in heaven) means taking God at his word in Christ. Not the act of a moment only, it is the attitude of a whole life (Gal. 2.20). And the faith which commits us to Christ commits us also to his community. Moreover, such faith is meant of God to express itself in good works (Eph. 2.10).

Similarly, Forsyth defines faith as 'the grand venture in which we commit our whole soul and future to the confidence that Christ is not an illusion but the reality of God'. The same act in which we confess Christ as Saviour and Lord sets us in Christ's body, the church. And Christians he calls those who 'live by faith and work through love'.

In their concept of Christ as the God-man there is also common ground between the fifth evangelist and Forsyth. Both speak of Christ's self-emptying (*kenōsis*) in the incarnation. (Compare Phil. 2.6–11 and I Cor. 8.9 with what Forsyth says in chapter 11 of his book *The Person and Place of Jesus Christ*, though Forsyth adds to the diminuendo of the *kenōsis* a corresponding crescendo of *plerōsis*, or 'fulfilment'). If Paul says that 'in Christ dwells the fullness of the Godhead bodily' (Col. 2.9), Forsyth affirms that in Christ we have 'the reality of God, but not the whole of God'. And if Paul declares (in Colossians and Ephesians) that in Christ all creation coheres, as towards him all history converges, Forsyth asserts that the grace of God in Christ is 'the groundwork of the universe', as 'the spinal cord of history is redemption'.

Compare what Forsyth says in his book about preaching the gospel today with what Paul says in Rom. 1.16 and II Cor. 5.18–20, and you cannot mistake how 'Pauline' he is.[9] For both, the proclamation of the word is an act continuing God's saving work in Christ and conveying it. 'The gospel prolonging and declaring itself', is how Forsyth defines preaching. It is the dynamic medium through which God contemporizes his historic

10

revelation in Christ and offers men the chance of responding to it by faith.

What of their teaching on the last things? It cannot be claimed that Forsyth shared all Paul's varying views here. (To some of us it seems clear that Paul grew in eschatological insight as he grew in grace. Compare the eschatology of his prison letters with that of the two early epistles to the Thessalonians.)

For Forsyth, our statements about the last things are essentially 'transpositions into the key of the hereafter' of that saving knowledge of God which we already have in Christ and the cross.[10] But on the central issue – that in the end God will triumph over all evil, wind up the scroll of history, and consummate in heaven the salvation he began in Christ – Paul and Forsyth agree. Nor do they disagree about the nature of the life to come. For both, Christian immortality is the gift of God in the risen and regnant Christ, as for both God will hereafter give his saints spiritual bodies – bodies suited to the conditions of the next world as our present physical ones are suited to the conditions of this. Like Paul in I Cor. 15, Forsyth declares: 'What happens to our physical body is a matter of indifference to faith', since our hope is set not on 'a resurrection of relics' (cf. I Cor. 15.50) but on a God-given spiritual organism. For the rest, Forsyth is at one with the apostle who wrote the chapter which begins with 'no condemnation' and ends with 'no separation': 'What then shall we say to these things? If God be for us, who can be against us? He that spared not his own Son, but delivered him up for us all, how shall he not with him freely give us all things? . . . For I am persuaded, that neither death, nor life, nor angels nor principalities, nor powers, nor things present, nor things to come, nor height nor depth, nor any other creature, shall be able to separate us from the love of God which is in Christ Jesus our Lord' (Rom. 8.31f., 37ff.).

Forsyth is now acknowledged to rank among the great theologians of the twentieth century.[11] 'But how much he owes to the church's earliest theologian, the 'man in Christ' who, in the dawn of Christianity, did more than any other to set Christ's holy fire

11

blazing in the earth and to change the course of history! Well did Forsyth name him 'the fifth evangelist'.

'Half gospels,' he wrote in a characteristic sentence, 'have no dignity and no future. Like the famous mule, they have neither pride of ancestry nor hope of posterity.' By no stretch of the imagination could Forsyth's gospel, firm-based as it was on St Paul's, be described as a half gospel. Is not this the gospel which the heralds of Christ ought to be proclaiming today to a bewildered and sin-sick world?

2

Paul as Writer

Is there any writer of whom Buffon's 'the style is the man' is truer than of St Paul? For the apostle, letter-writing was a substitute for personal action; and when he took his pen in hand or dictated to an amanuensis like Tertius (Rom. 16.22), the whole man – all his energy, passion, pride and tenderness – went down on the papyrus sheet.

Paul's writing does not smell of the lamp or show traces of 'the laborious file'. He does not construct his sentences with the fastidious care of a Plato. Yet his Greek is far above the artless common Greek to be found in the contemporary papyrus documents which archaeologists not long ago exhumed from the sands of old Egypt. The reason is simple: if Paul was not a university graduate, he was a man of excellent education, an education which owed a great deal to Judaism and not a little to Hellenism. So we get the paradox that, though Paul is, in Gilbert Murray's words, 'one of the great figures of Greek literature', a great classical scholar like Norden freely confessed, 'Paul is a writer whom I at least only understand with great difficulty'.

What puzzled Norden in Paul's Greek was doubtless its Semitic undertone, the fact that many of his Greek words (e.g. *dikaiosunē*, righteousness, *eleos*, mercy, and *alētheia*, truth) are stained with Hebrew meanings.[12] In fact, Paul's letters are as full of subconscious echoes of the Greek Old Testament (the Septuagint) as Bunyan's *Pilgrim's Progress* is replete with echoes of the King James Bible.

As for public speaking, Paul confesses that he is an amateur (*idiotēs*, II Cor. 11.6), and disclaims reliance on the orator's techniques of persuasion: 'My speech and my message,' he writes

(I Cor. 2.4), 'were not in plausible words of wisdom but in demonstration of the Spirit and of power.' But we must take this self-estimate as a speaker with a grain of salt, if only for the very good reason that, judged by results, he was a mightily effective one. Yet, though Paul disdained the devices of the rhetorician, his letters contain much more art than appears at first sight. Take, for example, this passage from Rom. 14.7f.:

> None of us lives to himself, and none of us dies to himself.
> If we live, we live to the Lord, and if we die, we die to the Lord;
> So then, whether we live or whether we die, we are the Lord's.
> For to this end Christ died and lived again,
> That he might be Lord both of the dead and of the living.

Such symmetrical parallelism, with its rhythm and cadence, shows as much artistry as a lyric of Burns (himself no illiterate ploughman). But beyond question the finest example is Paul's 'Song of Songs' in I Cor. 13. We print it usually as prose, but it is certainly poetry and ought always to be printed as it is in Moffatt's translation:

> I may speak with the tongues of men and of angels,
> > but if I have no love,
> > > I am a noisy gong or a clanging cymbal;
> I may prophesy, fathom all mysteries and secret lore,
> I may have such absolute faith that I can move
> > hills from their place,
> > but if I have no love,
> > > I count for nothing;
> I may distribute all I possess in charity,
> I may give up my body to be burnt,
> > but if I have no love,
> > > I make nothing of it.

Observe the choice of words, the figures of speech, the rhythm of the whole stanza. This artistry, surely not unconscious, plus the fact that the passage fits very loosely into the context, strongly suggests that Paul did not compose it in the flowering instant.

Johannes Weiss, the great German scholar, was probably right when he called it a deliberate creation – created like a poem by his own countryman Goethe.

Now let us try to characterize Paul as a writer in more depth and detail.

To begin with, let us contrast him with St John. Mersch, the Roman Catholic theologian, has done it for us:

> Paul was converted in the way that best suits the character of Paul. The Word of God leaped forth on him like a robber, and in consequence there remained an element of aggressiveness and abruptness even in his style. St John was of a different stamp, and God won him as befitted John. The truth unveiled itself within his soul, as a summer landscape rises before one's eyes at eventide.

The 'abruptness' to which Mersch refers finds illustration in Paul's fondness for pointed contrasts. Training may have something to do with this, but so also must Paul's temperament – he had one of these 'either-or' natures – as well as his experience – his conversion had cut his life in two. At any rate he was a master of antithesis. Romans 6.23 yields a splendid short example: 'Sin's wage is death, but God's gift is life eternal in Christ Jesus our Lord.' For a longer but no less memorable one we may turn to I Cor. 15.42f., where Paul is seeking to describe the nature of the spiritual body which God will hereafter give those who are 'in Christ':

> What is sown is mortal,
> What rises is immortal.
> Sown inglorious,
> It rises in glory;
> Sown in weakness,
> It rises in power;
> Sown an animate body,
> It rises a spiritual body.

Consider, next, Paul's use of the diatribe style in argument.

15

Nowadays a diatribe means an invective harangue. In Paul's day it meant the kind of disputation which itinerant Stoic preachers had popularized in their street-corner sermons: and no doubt Paul had often heard them at it. The speaker would conjure up an imaginary opponent – in Rom. 2 and 3 it is 'the Jewish objector' – and argue the case with him. He, the objector, raises a difficulty ('Then what advantage has the Jew?', Rom. 3.1) and in his reply the speaker demolishes the objection – and his critic with it. For an example, take I Cor. 15.35f.: 'But someone will ask, How are the dead raised?' 'How foolish! The seed you sow does not come to life unless it has first died.' Oftener, however, Paul's rejoinder is a brief but emphatic 'No, never!' (or, as the AV translates it 'God forbid!'). Thus, in Gal. 2.17, 'Does that mean that Christ is an abettor of sin? No, never!'

A third feature of Paul's style is his love of metaphor. In this he is a true oriental, delighting in picture-language, and drawing his figures from various aspects of life.

Agriculture gives him: 'I planted the seed, and Apollos watered it, but God made it grow' (I Cor. 3.6), as, a few verses later, architecture supplies him with: 'Like a skilled master-builder I laid the foundation.' Military metaphors abound in Paul's pages: 'If the trumpet-call is not clear, who will prepare for battle?' (I Cor. 14.8); 'Put on the whole armour of God' (Eph. 6.11); 'the weapons of our warfare are not worldly' (II Cor. 10.4); 'the peace of God will garrison your hearts' (Phil. 4.7).

No less common are athletic metaphors, with the stadium and the arena forming the background: 'Run to win!' (I Cor. 9.24); 'I press on toward the goal for the prize' (Phil. 3.14); 'We wrestle not with flesh and blood' (Eph. 6.12); 'I am like a boxer who does not beat the air; I bruise my own body and make it know its master, for fear that after preaching to others I should find myself rejected' (I Cor. 9.26f.).

Not surprisingly, Paul the Roman citizen raids politics for a few images: 'Our capital city (*politeuma*)', he tells the Philippians, 'is in heaven' (Phil. 3.20). 'You are no longer aliens in a foreign land,' he assures the Gentiles, 'but fellow-citizens with God's people' (Eph. 2.19). 'So then we are ambassadors for Christ,' he writes to the Corinthians (II Cor. 5.20).

Similarly, the business world of buying and selling furnishes him with metaphors. 'All I care for,' he tells the Philippians, 'is the profit accruing to your credit' (Phil. 4.17). We apostles, he reminds the Corinthians, 'are not peddlers of God's word, as so many are' (II Cor. 2.17). And thrice in his letters he describes the Holy Spirit indwelling Christian hearts as the 'arles' (*arrabōn*), i.e. the first instalment, or down payment, of their heavenly inheritance (II Cor. 1.22; 5.5; Eph. 1.14).

When we recall that every second man on the streets of Ephesus or Corinth was a slave, it is not surprising to find Paul often describing sin as slavery or salvation as emancipation. Common also in his letters are figures and images drawn from domestic and family life. Thus, he tells the Galatians that the Law has been our *paidagōgos*, i.e. the domestic (slave) guardian-cum-tutor, to bring us to Christ (Gal. 3.24). Not only are Christians 'members of the household of faith' (Gal. 6.10), but they are the adopted sons of God (Gal. 4.5; Rom. 8.15; Eph. 1.5), and their destiny is to be 'shaped to the likeness of God's Son, that he might be the eldest among a large family of brothers' (Rom. 8.29).

Sacrificial metaphors also are frequent. Writing of the cross he tells the Romans that 'God designed Christ to be the means of expiating sin by his sacrificial death, effective through faith' (Rom. 3.25). Or again, in Eph. 5.2, he writes of our Lord's atoning death thus: 'Christ gave himself up on your behalf as an offering and sacrifice whose fragrance is pleasing to God.' Or, bidding the Corinthians 'purge out' the bad leaven in their fellowship, he says: 'Our Passover has begun: the sacrifice is offered – Christ himself' (I Cor. 5.7).

Nor must we forget Paul's legal metaphors, bound up as they are with his teaching in Romans and Galatians about 'justification by faith'. God's forgiveness of sinners for Christ's sake he describes as a law-court acquittal. Daringly he depicts him as a judge who acquits guilty men (Rom. 4.5), so that 'now there is no condemnation for those who are in (union with) Christ Jesus'.

Yet perhaps Paul's most famous metaphor is anatomical. 'You

are the body of Christ, and, individually, members of it' (I Cor. 12.27), a metaphor so influential in Christian thinking down the centuries that one modern theologian has even made it the key to Paul's theology.[13]

Faults in plenty Paul has as a writer. Occasionally he can be as obscure as the poet Browning at his worst. (An example will be found in Gal. 2.3ff. To this day we cannot be quite sure whether Titus was circumcised or not.) In Phil. 2.1 he apparently commits a solecism. Sometimes he is guilty of what the grammarians call *anacoluthia* – want of syntactical sequence, as when the latter part of the sentence does not grammatically fit the earlier, as, for example, in Rom. 5.12–14. But these inconcinnities are mere spots on the sun. They are the faults of a man in great haste on his Lord's business: you do not stop to polish your phrases when your converts are resiling from the grace of God (as in Galatia) or downing tools to scan the sky for a returning Christ (as in Thessalonica), or getting drunk at the Holy Communion (as at Corinth).

All in all, as a writer he shows astonishing versatility. How different, for example, is his magnum opus, Romans, from his little private letter to Philemon about his runaway slave Onesimus! The differences are partly due to the subject matter and the circumstances which occasioned the letters, but partly also to the man who can change his tone and become all things to all men. All his varying moods are reflected in his correspondence: anger (Gal. 3.1), grief (Rom. 9.3), pride (II Cor. 11.5), defiance (Gal. 6.17), irony (I Cor. 4.8–10) and, of course, affection (Phil. 4.1).

Paul's is 'the style of genius if not the genius of style'. If he rises to great heights, it is not because he has spent long hours prettifying his periods, but because, as in I Cor. 3.21f., he is overmastered by the greatness of the gospel: 'For all things are yours, whether Paul, or Apollos, or Cephas, or the world, or life, or death, or the present, or the future, all are yours, and you are Christ's, and Christ is God's'; or, because, as in II Cor. 6.8f., he is both humbled and exalted by a sense of his high calling as one of Christ's apostles:

> Honour and dishonour, praise and blame, are alike our lot: we are the impostors who speak the truth, the unknown men whom all men know; dying we still live on; disciplined by suffering, we are not done to death; in our sorrows we have always cause for joy; poor ourselves, we bring wealth to many; penniless, we own the world (NEB).

The saying of Longinus that 'sublimity is the echo of a great soul' finds no better illustration than the man who penned the imperishable hymn about Christian love, 'the great and comfortable words' concerning the resurrection, and that majestic chapter in his Romans which begins with 'no condemnation' and ends with 'no separation'. T. R. Glover wrote:

> Every sentence comes charged with the whole man. Half a dozen Greek words – and not always the best Greek – and the Christian world will for ever sum up its deepest experience in, 'God forbid that I should glory save in the cross of our Lord Jesus Christ, by whom the world is crucified unto me and I unto the world'.[14]

3

Paul as Liberator

Paul's letter to the Galatians (possibly his earliest epistle) is the first sword-stroke in a battle for what, centuries later, Martin Luther (whose favourite epistle it was) called 'the liberty of the Christian man'.

Even in a modern version, it is not an easy letter to read; and sometimes, as in his forced allegory about Hagar and Sarah (4.21–31) or his use of the word 'seed' (3.16), his arguments leave the modern reader cold. Yet, like other people's arguments today, Paul's are less important than the conclusion which he uses them to reach – that we must never let the freedom of the gospel of Christ get tangled up with Jewish legalism. For the rest, the difficulties or obscurities in Galatians are the faults of a man zealous for the truth of the gospel and in great haste on the Lord's business. When your beloved converts are resiling from the grace of God and you are 'at your wits' end' (Gal. 4.20, NEB) about them, you don't mince your words or stop to polish your phrases. Such was Paul's situation and concern.

But who were these Galatians, and what cardinal principle of Christianity was at stake when Paul wrote to them?

As Sir William Ramsay, a great expert on Asia Minor, showed, they were almost certainly the dwellers in the *Roman province* of Galatia, that is, the people in Derbe, Lystra, Iconium, etc., whom Paul and Barnabas had evangelized on their missionary journey (see Acts 13–14), probably in the years AD 47–48.

Some time after the two apostles had said goodbye to their Galatian converts there had come among them some Jewish Christians – 'Judaizers' we call them, for short – telling them that, if they wanted to become proper Christians, they must submit to circumcision and keep the Law of Moses: in other words, become Jews before they became Christians.

Paul, these Judaizers insinuated, was only a second-hand apostle, having derived his knowledge of Christ from Peter and the original apostles in Jerusalem. Besides, he was a trimmer, or men-pleaser, saying one thing here and another thing there, where the Law was concerned.

When news reached Paul that his converts in Galatia had fallen for this Judaized caricature of the gospel, understandably he saw red. 'I am astonished to find you turning so quickly away from him who called you by his grace,' he wrote, 'You gormless Galatians, who has cast his spell on you?' (Read Galatians in a modern translation, and you will understand why men, like J. B. Phillips, when turning the letter into contemporary English, have felt 'like men re-wiring an old house with the mains turned on'.)

Galatians has six chapters. The first two are *autobiographical*. In them Paul defends his gospel and his credentials as an apostle.

To refute the slanders of the Judaizers, he tells the story of his spiritual life: how once as a perfervid Pharisee he had thought it his duty to persecute the Christians until that memorable day on the Damascus Road, when God had revealed his risen Son to him and called him to be an apostle, or special messenger, to the Gentiles; how, on later visits to Jerusalem, the 'pillar' apostles there had acknowledged his apostleship, endorsed the gospel he preached, and approved his mission to the Gentiles; how later still, at Antioch in Syria, he had been forced to rebuke even Peter himself for betraying what he knew to be the liberty of the gospel and leading others astray.

In chapters 3 and 4, which are *biblical and doctrinal*, Paul makes three appeals to his readers.

First, to their religious experience. 'Was it by observing the Law,' he asks, 'or by believing the gospel that you received the gift of God's Spirit and all those wonderful experiences of his grace? Answer me, honestly.'

Second, to scripture. 'Go back to Genesis,' Paul says, 'and you will see that it was not by Law-keeping that Abraham, the father of the faithful, found acceptance with God. Abraham, we read, put his faith in God, and that faith was counted to him for righteousness. More, it was for this faith that he got the divine promise that in his offspring all nations would be blessed. So, it is men of faith who are God's true sons and heirs of the promise. Scripture itself says that trying to save yourself by Law-keeping only brings curse and condemnation, since no man can fully keep the Law. From that curse Christ bought us freedom when, on his cross, God made him a curse for us. The Law, coming four centuries later, was a parenthetical dispensation, to serve a temporary purpose – to deepen the sense of sin by exposing it as transgression.

'Think of the Law as a tutor in charge of us until Christ should come, and by faith in him we might get right with God. Once we were like the heir to an estate while still a minor. Kept under ward, his status differs little from a slave's. But a day dawns when he comes of age and into his inheritance. So we once lived in bondage to false gods. But when his appointed time came, God sent his own Son, born under the Law, to deliver us from our bondage and make us his adopted sons. And the proof that in union with Christ we are such, is his Holy Spirit in our hearts moving us to cry "Abba! Father!" Why then do you want to revert to that slavery from which Christ has set you free?'

Paul's third appeal is to the time when he had first gone among them with the gospel. Then they had welcomed him, sick man though he was, as a messenger from heaven for whom they would have plucked out their very eyes. 'What has come over you,' Paul cries, 'O my little children, must I be in birth-pangs all over again till Christ take shape in you?'

In chapters 5 and 6, which are *practical*, Paul says: 'The freedom Christ has won for you never surrender. To submit to circumcision and try to make yourself right with God by Law-keeping is to sever your connection with Christ and fall from divine grace. The one thing needful is faith working through love. In spite of your fall, whoever caused it, I am confident you will still run well. But, as free men, never let your liberty become a licence to indulge your lower nature with all its evil impulses. Serve one another with that love which sums up the whole Law. The way to overcome your lower nature is to let God's Spirit take control and bring forth in you all his gracious fruits.

'If a man does something wrong, correct him gently, for none of us is immune to temptation. and help to bear each other's burdens: so you will fulfil the law of Christ.[15] God is not fooled. As a man sows, he reaps. Sow to your lower nature and you will reap a fatal harvest. Sow in the Spirit's field, and you will reap eternal life. Therefore never tire of doing good.

'Here is my parting word to you, written in my own bold capitals. The sole aim of these circumcising brethren is to glory in the number of their converts and escape persecution for the cross of Christ. But God forbid that I should glory in anything but that cross which has changed my whole world completely. Circumcision is nothing; uncircumcision is nothing; the only thing that counts is men recreated in union with Christ. From now on let no man make trouble for me, for I carry on my scarred body the marks of my owner, Jesus. His grace be with you all.'

The main question in Galatians is: how does a man become a Christian – by works of Law or by faith in Christ?

Originally, works of Law meant devotion to God as expressed in the Ten Commandments. But, by Paul's day, the Jewish religion had, like Molière's ghost, improved very much for the worse. As their professional theologians, the Scribes, kept 'fencing the Law', i.e. interpreting and re-applying it in detail to all sorts of situations, the number of the 'Thou shalts' or 'Thou shalt nots' had grown into several hundreds. Instead of heart-to-heart communion with God, religion had become the observance of a host of pettifogging rules and regulations, on the keeping of which man's salvation depended. God had been turned into a great taskmaster whose rules were hard to remember and harder yet to practise. And if, like Paul, you were a very earnest Pharisee, you were likely to end up, as he did – see Rom. 7.24 – with a cry of utter despair.

23

Here we may recall that Jesus had condemned the Scribes and Pharisees for binding grievous legal burdens on men's shoulders, getting their moral priorities all wrong, and shutting people out of God's kingdom (Matt. 23). 'Away with this hypocrisy', he had said, 'the whole Law can be summed up in two commandments – Love God, and love your neighbour' (Mark 12.29–31). 'Come to me, all who are labouring under the Law's heavy burdens, take my yoke upon you and learn from me, and I will give you rest' (Matt. 11.28ff.). And, when Paul met the risen Christ, he found all this was true: salvation was by faith in Christ, and not by works of Law. But if such faith is God's gracious gift in Christ, does this mean that 'good works' no longer matter? On the contrary, as Paul explains elsewhere (Eph. 2.8–10), we are 'Gods handiwork' created in Christ for the doing of good deeds. Such deeds, however, are no longer deeds done to secure a reward; they are deeds done because of a gift already received. True goodness springs from a transformed heart, so that a Christian man or woman does good almost mechanically.

By faith or by works? Is not this just an ancient controversy now as dead as the dodo? On the contrary, in one form or another, it keeps recurring in church history. Ask many a modern man what Christianity means to him, and his answer will not be unlike the Pharisee's in Christ's parable (Luke 18.9–14): 'I keep the Ten Commandments – or most of them. I'm not a thief or an adulterer. I don't cheat in business or injure other people. I may not observe Lent or tithe my income for support of the church. But I respect religion – why, I even go to Holy Communion twice a year. So I'm quite happy with my little code of rules, and at the Last Judgment – if there is one – I don't think the Almighty will have much against me.'

Is not this, basically, the modern version of salvation by works – a few works at any rate? If Paul were among us today, would he not so have described it?

What makes a man a real Christian? Is it rules and regulations? Or is it that self-commitment to God through Christ his Son which is called faith? Codes of conduct, the observance of rules and regulations, may have their place in life and their function may not be so negative as Paul supposes. The trouble is that they do not really go to the root of the spiritual matter. True change of heart in a man can never be effected by regulating conduct from without. At best, all it will produce is a tamed animal – not a new man. What is needed to change a man's heart is what Thomas Chalmers called 'the expulsive power of a new affection' – falling in love with God's Saviour Son, and staying in love with him, and serving others in love for his sake, till you can say with something of the great simplicity of Paul, 'The life I now live in the flesh I live by faith in the Son of God, who loved me and gave himself for me' (Gal. 2.20). This it is which makes a man a real Christian.

In Galatians, then, Paul was contending for the very truth and liberty of the gospel. If he had lost the battle, conceivably the gospel might have been put into a Jewish strait-jacket. Christianity might have dwindled into a heretical sect of Judaism, and Paul's vision of a world-wide church become an empty dream.

Nor is 'the epistle of Christian freedom' a dead letter today. Soul-destroying legalism of one sort or another can still rear its ugly head in the church of Christ. When this happens – whenever the observance of a code of pettifogging rules and regulations is set on a level with faith in God's Christ as a means of salvation – Galatians can again become (what it was in Luther's hands at the Reformation) a sword of the spirit to strike the error down. Christ's is the only name given under heaven whereby men may be saved from their sin; and trust in him as Saviour – a trust that works through love – the only way of salvation.

Paul as Pastor

Imagine, if you can, a compound of London, New York and Paris with a bit of Port Said thrown in, and you will have some idea of what the ancient city of Corinth was like. To gather a Christian flock in such a cosmopolitan seaport must have been like trying to set up the City of God in Vanity Fair. For the city, to which Paul had brought the gospel in AD 50, was then a byword for permissiveness, as to 'Corinthianize' was polite Greek for to go to the devil with women.[16]

Yet in that city Paul had succeeded in planting a vigorous outpost of the church, and after his departure along had come Apollos, the brilliant preacher from Alexandria, to continue his work. 'I planted the seed in God's field,' Paul writes, 'and Apollos watered it, but God made it grow' (I Cor. 3.5). Now, however, five years later, weeds had begun to appear among the wheat. Some Christian travellers from Corinth reported to Paul, then working in Ephesus (I Cor. 16.8), that ugly factions were splitting the church in Corinth, there was evidence of immorality, and some church members were taking their quarrels before pagan judges.

About the same time Paul had received a rather complacent letter from the Corinthian church itself, inviting his judgment on various problems, among them Christian marriage to unbelievers and the morality of eating meat which had originally been consecrated to heathen idols.

I Corinthians is Paul's answer to the matters in the report and the questions raised in the church letter. Here is the New English Bible's analysis of its contents:

After giving thanks for the blessings which the gospel had brought to Corinth, Paul turns at once to their reported party strife and their various slogans: 'I am for Paul', 'I am for Peter', 'I am for Apollos'. 'Has Christ been parcelled out?' he asks indignantly, 'Was Paul crucified for you?' Wise men you may think yourselves, but, as the cross shows, God's wisdom is not man's, as witness the fact that you have been called – you who can make no pretence to wisdom or noble birth. There *is* a wisdom God gives to men who possess his Holy Spirit. But when you tolerate these factions in your fellowship, you show how unspiritual you are.

One foundation only is there for Christian faith, Jesus Christ; and we apostles, building on it, are accountable to God for how we build. Therefore stop exalting one human leader against another! And please to remember what your vaunted spiritual triumphs are costing us apostles in hardship and contempt from men.

Many Christian teachers you may have but only one father-in-God; and when I revisit you, it will be for you to decide whether our reunion is fierce or friendly.

I was shocked to hear about this Christian living in sin with his father's wife. For his own eternal good you must expel him from your fellowship.

As for those church members who are taking their private quarrels into heathen law-courts, surely you ought to settle such matters in your own fellowship? Isn't there a single wise man among you able to give a decision in a brother-Christian's case? Better still, why not suffer injury without going to law at all (1–6)?

Then, at chapter 7, Paul adverts to the questions in the church's

27

letter. The first was about marriage: 'To marry or not to marry when the world's end may not be far away? May a Christian seek divorce if his life's partner is a pagan?'

'In this present distressful time,' Paul answers, 'stay unmarried, like myself, if you can. If not, marry. Better to marry than burn with passion! To the married I give this commandment (not my own but Christ's): there must be no divorce. If a Christian has a pagan wife (and the same applies to a Christian wife with a heathen husband), he should not divorce her; for the heathen wife belongs to God through her Christian husband, as do any children born to them. On the other hand, if the heathen partner is set on a divorce, so be it. God's call to us is a call to live in peace. One further point: if her husband dies, a Christian wife is free to re-marry. But, for myself, I think she is better off as she is.'

The Corinthians' next question was: 'May a Christian eat meats which have been consecrated to heathen idols (as most of the meat on sale in their markets had been)?'

'All things may be lawful,' Paul answers, 'but not all things are advisable. Of course these heathen idols have no real existence – there is only one God and one Saviour. Yet, for the sake of your weaker brothers who have not full knowledge you must take care how you use this freedom, or you may be the cause of your weaker brother's downfall. You may harm him by doing something which otherwise is not really wrong. He may think your eating of such meat a justification of idolatry.

'Take my own case. As Christ's apostle I have as much right as any other apostle to marry and live off the church. Yet, rather than hinder the gospel, I have not exercised it. Christ said that those who preach the gospel should get their living from it. Yet I have not done so. In my evangelism I am simply discharging a trust laid upon me. Alas for me if I do not preach the gospel! Ever my aim has been to save as many as possible, be they Jews or Gentiles.' 'You Corinthians,' Paul proceeds, 'must not suppose that because you have the sacraments you can safely eat sacrificial meat. The Israelites in the wilderness had their sacraments also. Yet that did not prevent God from punishing their idol-

28

worship. Therefore shun idolatry. Consider what happens at the Lord's supper. When we bless the "cup of blessing", is it not a means of sharing in the blood of Christ? And when we break the bread, is it not a means of sharing in his body? This is why it is dangerous to suppose that you can safely partake of both the Lord's table and that of demons.

'You say. "We are free to do anything." Yes, but is everything good for us? Does everything help to build up God's people, the church? Therefore let everyone seek not his own but his brother's good; and whether you eat or drink, do all to the glory of God.'

The next Corinthian question was: 'Should women have their heads covered at public worship?' 'Yes,' Paul replies, 'the veil symbolizes woman's subordination to man. Judge for yourselves: is it fitting for a woman to pray to God bare-headed? Do not both nature and church custom tell you No?'

'I am informed,' Paul goes on, 'that at your common meal before communion some richer members are gorging themselves and getting drunk while their poorer brothers, arriving late from their work, have to go hungry.

'Such behaviour I cannot praise. I would remind you that this is the *Lord's* supper. As I taught you, our common meal goes back to what Christ did in the upper room on the night he was betrayed. Unless you have a reverent sense of what you are doing at it, your communions may bring down God's judgment on you' (7–11).

'Now about those spiritual gifts in which you are so rich. I would remind you that they all come from the one Spirit who indwells the body of Christ, as each of them is given for the common good. In a human body no rivalry exists among the various organs: each has its own function to perform. So it is in Christ's church: one man's special gift may be for prophecy (inspired preaching), another's for teaching, another's for healing, another's for administration, and so on. All are needed, but aim at the higher gifts. The best of all is *agapē* – Christian love. Without this, the rest are nothing worth. Gifts like prophecy and "tongues" (*glōssolalia*, i.e. ecstatic speech under stress of religious emotion) will come to an end. Faith, hope and love abide, the last being greatest of all.

'So make love your aim, but earnestly desire spiritual gifts, especially prophecy. The prophet is worth more than the man who speaks in tongues. Tongues benefit only their possessor – unless someone is present who can interpret their meaning and so help to build up the congregation. Otherwise, his words will sound like gibberish. God be thanked, I can speak in such tongues more than any of you; but, in church, I would rather utter five intelligible words with my mind than ten thousand in a tongue.

'Be grown-up in your thinking. If, the congregation being assembled, all are heard speaking with tongues as outsiders come in, will they not conclude that you are off your heads? Therefore, at your worship, no more than two or three of these ecstatic speakers, and one at a time. If no interpreter is present, let them keep quiet afterwards. So with prophets: let two or three of them speak – again, one at a time – and let the rest of the worshippers weigh well what they say. Women should not be allowed to speak in church: if there is something they want to know, let them ask their husbands at home. In short, be keen to prophesy, don't forbid ecstatic utterance; but, above all, let everything be done decently and in order' (12–14).

Finally, Paul takes up the question of life after death. 'Some of you, I hear, while not denying Christ's resurrection, cannot believe in bodily resurrection of men. Evidently you have not grasped the significance of Christ's victory over death. Were bodily resurrection impossible, there could be no risen Christ. A dead Saviour cannot save you. You would be still be in your sins.

'In fact, he is risen and alive. As by a man came death, by a man also has come resurrection from the dead. As in Adam all die, so also in union with Christ shall all be made alive, when, finally, he hands over the sovereignty to his Father; for he must reign till God has put all his enemies under his feet, the last being death itself.

'But (you ask) in what kind of body will the dead be raised?

30

It will be a spiritual body – a frame suitable to the heavenly world. Take, for illustration, a seed. To live again, it must first die; but it lives again, not in the old body but in a new God-given one. (Are there not heavenly and earthly bodies, and does the sun have a splendour of its own, and the stars yet another?) So it will be with our resurrection. What is sown is mortal, what rises is immortal. Sown an animate body, it rises a spiritual one. As we have worn the likeness of the man of dust, so shall we wear the likeness of the heavenly man.

'Flesh and blood can never inherit the heavenly world. When God consummates his kingdom, the dead will rise, and we shall all be changed; for this corruptible must put on incorruption, and this mortal immortality. God be praised who gives us the victory through our Lord Jesus Christ!

'On, therefore, with the Lord's work, unwearyingly, assured that such labour can never be lost!' (15).

Such, less chapter 16, which is about Paul's travel plans and his collection for the poor Christians in Jerusalem, is Paul's pastoral letter.

How shall we appraise Paul as pastor in I Corinthians? In some ways he is clearly a man of his time. Thus, for example, in chapter 7 he is convinced that the end of the world is not far away, so that his advices here are in the nature of interim-ethics. In this belief Paul was mistaken. Still today the time of the world's end remains as it was in Christ's day (Mark 13.32), a reserved secret in the breast of God.

Again, when he says that women's heads should be covered at worship and that they should not be allowed to speak in church, he exposes himself to the 'Women's Lib' charge of being a first-century male chauvinist.

In matters like these many Christians nowadays think differently. But, when we moderns are minded to criticize Paul, we should never forget that he was facing, almost single-handed, many quite new problems and had not at his back the accumulated wisdom of long centuries of Christian experience. Further, remembering 'the care of all the churches' (II Cor. 11.28) which weighed on Paul daily, should we not mix our criticism of the apostle with a modicum of the charity which he himself recommended?

On the other hand, how much more there is to be said on the credit side and in Paul's clear favour! Stern, Paul could be, as when denouncing factions in the church or flagrant immorality; but so ought every true pastor be today. Yet through all his admonitions there always shines a deep love for his 'parishioners', so that one feels indeed how truly he is father as well as founder of the church at Corinth. More, does he not repeatedly reveal in his letter much practical sagacity as well as a faculty for distinguishing between essentials and non-essentials? Again and again, to problems of Christian behaviour he brings a sanctified common sense, as when he reminds the Corinthian libertarians that 'liberty is the luxury of self-discipline' or seeks to introduce decency and order into the wild confusion of their worship. That he was also a very businesslike man of God appears in the closing chapter when he directs his readers every Lord's Day to set aside money for 'Christian aid' to their poorer brethren in the mother church at Jerusalem.

Every good pastor, besides being a wise shepherd to his flock, should be something of a theologian with a firm grip on the basics of the gospel and an ability to instruct his people in its moral issues. If we judge Paul on these counts, has there ever been in Christian history an abler 'ecumenical' pastor than St Paul? (Another such, though on a smaller scale, was John Wesley in the eighteenth century.)

For the rest, so long as Christendom lasts, Christians will give thanks for the man who gave them his 'Song of Songs' in praise of Christian love and his 'great and comfortable words' about the resurrection.

5

Paul as Theologian

'The chief book of the New Testament and the purest gospel', said Martin Luther. 'The most profound work in existence,' declared S. T. Coleridge. 'The most important theological book ever written,' says John Knox, the distinguished American theologian.

These are tremendous claims to make for a letter written 1900 years ago by a little Jewish tent-maker in a back street of Corinth. You may think them unwarranted or, at any rate, overstated. Yet it is mere matter of history that Romans has been a letter of destiny. In century after century the spiritual fire which lies at its core has blazed out afresh as one great Christian after another – a Luther, a Wesley, a Barth – has kindled his torch at it for the good of the whole church.

In his reforming zeal Luther made bold to say that 'every Christian should have Romans by heart and take it about with him as the daily bread of his soul'. Alas, today, how many Christians ever open the book? Nor are they altogether to be blamed. Without a good commentary (and there is no lack of these), Romans is hard going, especially if you read it in the archaic (if glorious) English of the Authorized Version. (Here the New English Bible can illumine many dark places.) But it is not only the language of Romans which perplexes many; they are not a little mystified by its theology, which seems to them to have little bearing on their daily life or the problems which vex mankind today.

Romans is indeed full of theology. But what, after all, is theology but 'faith thinking' – faith giving a reasoned account of itself. And in his letter Paul is doing just this. Romans is, in fact, the answer to the question, 'What is Christianity?' by the greatest thinker in the early church: and what Paul has to say in it is very much our concern today.

Paul wrote Romans about AD 57, in order to pave the way for his long-intended visit to Rome. He wrote *urbi* – to the city called Rome. Unwittingly, he also wrote *orbi* – to the world, as history has proved.

Romans has sixteen chapters. The last one, which is mostly a list of Christians in Rome known to Paul, we can here omit. For our purposes we may also dwell briefly on chapters 9–11 (which Paul may have composed earlier and incorporated here).[17] It deals with what we may call the Jewish question, i.e. the problem over which Paul had long agonized: 'Why have the Jews, God's chosen people – and my own people – rejected Jesus their Messiah and apparently excluded themselves from God's grace?' First (9), looking at the matter from the divine side, he says in effect: 'God is sovereign and may do as he wills. If some Jews have fallen out of his favour, it was always God's purpose to include Gentiles among his people.' Next (10), he surveys things from the human angle, arguing: 'If for the present the Jews have missed salvation, it is because they have themselves gone the wrong way about it, seeking to save themselves by "works", and rejecting the good news of God's grace in Christ.' But (11) he cannot rest in this sad conclusion, and in his last word on the subject, he holds out the hope that old Israel will yet be saved when God completes his saving purpose for a world of sinners. And he breaks out into a doxology: 'O the depth of the riches and wisdom and knowledge of God! How unsearchable are his judgments and how inscrutable his ways! For from him, and through him, and to him, are all things. To him be glory for ever. Amen.'

Now let us focus on chapters 1–8 and 12–15, which contain the heart of the gospel according to St Paul.

After greeting his readers, Paul tells them of his long-cherished desire to visit Rome. 'I am not ashamed of the Gospel,' he says; 'to the man with faith it is God's power for saving sinners.' And

Rome, he implies, has no lack of these. From this point on we may divide Romans into three parts:

1. The sin of man (1.17–3.20)
2. But the grace of God (3.21–8.39)
3. Therefore the Christian ethic (12.1–15.13).

In the gospel, Paul begins, 'the righteousness of God is being revealed.' This is one of his key-phrases, well rendered in the NEB as 'God's way of righting wrong', since it describes not so much a divine attribute as a divine *activity* – God putting things right for his people.

Through long centuries Israel had prayed that God would so put things right and 'visit and redeem his people'. Now, says the apostle, in the events that make up the gospel story he is to be seen doing it.

But why is the righteousness of God needed? Because of the *un*righteousness of men. Before God, mankind is morally bankrupt. To be sure, all men have some knowledge of God since he has made a general revelation of himself to them in his creation. But the Gentiles, rejecting this knowledge, have turned idolators. When men do this, God gives them up to the dire consequences of their sin. Hence the unnatural vice and depravity of the Gentile world we see around us.

But the Jews are in no better case. God has disclosed his nature and will for them in the Law of Moses, yet they have constantly flouted it. Though they pride themselves on having a special revelation of God in the Law, their actual behaviour – their disobedience to its commands – shows them no less guilty than the Gentiles.

Thus, in the sight of God, all men – Jews and Gentiles alike – are sinners, as the scriptures declare (1.17–3.20).

Such is the disease, sin wide as the world and deep as human nature.

At Rom. 3.21 Paul turns to the divine remedy. Now (he says) after, in his forebearance, overlooking men's sins in the past, God has begun to put things right for them. On his side, it is a matter of gracious giving, on man's of humble receiving. By works of Law – by strenuous moral endeavours to fulfil the Law's requirements – no man can put himself right with God (as the Pharisee in Christ's parable thought to do). But what man cannot do, God has now done for him in Christ. In the atoning cross God has provided a way for sinful man to be justified (3).

Such justification by faith is really as old as Abraham who obediently took God at his word and for it was counted right by God. Just so, Christian faith means taking God at his living Word in Christ – the Christ who, for our saving, died and rose again.

When we place our trust in him, God sets us right with himself, we have peace with him, our very hardships take on a new look, and we exult in hope of divine glory. As from Adam came sin and death for his descendants, so from Christ (the second Adam) have come forgiveness and new life for all who trust in him. For 'as through the disobedience of the one man many were made sinners, so through the obedience of the one man many will be made righteous.' (4–5). This new life means deliverance from sin's dominion, symbolized in baptism when we die with Christ to the old existence and rise into newness of life. No less it means rescue from the death-grip which the Law gets on us through sin's power in our lower nature (6).

Once, Paul confesses, I knew that experience only too well. Then, praise be to God, he rescued me through Christ. Thus, what the Law could not do, God has done in another way – through Christ and his cross (7).

So there is now no condemnation for those who are in union with Christ. What the Law, weakened by the flesh – our lower nature – could not do, God has done in Christ, and now we live in the power not of the flesh but of the Spirit. Led by the Spirit, we are no longer slaves but God's adopted sons, and heirs with Christ of his glory.

With that future glory our present suffering is not to be compared. As the creation shared in the blight of man's fall from grace, so it will also share in his final redemption. Meanwhile, the Holy Spirit assists us in our prayers, enabling us to cry

36

'Abba! Father', and God's elect may count on his cooperation in all that befalls them.

God is on our side. The Christ who died and rose again on our behalf, now intercedes for us in heaven. If God gave his only Son to save us, we may trust him to give us everything else we need, and nothing in the whole universe will be able to separate us from his invincible love (8).

Thus Paul ends his exposition of God's grace in Christ for sinners. But, if the gospel has a believing side to it, no less has it a behaving one. For the moral imperatives which the gospel lays on Christians we turn now to Rom. 12.1–15.13.

'As the recipients of God's grace,' Paul says, 'you must respond by living for God and your fellow-men in a quite new way. As members – or limbs – in Christ's body, the church, you are called to employ your various "grace-gifts" for the common good of God's people, whether it be preaching, teaching, administration, or helping others in distress. Love in all sincerity. Be aglow with the Spirit. Rejoice in hope, be patient in tribulation, be constant in prayer, practice hospitality. Bless those who persecute you. Never repay evil with evil, rather leave all retribution to the Lord. (How reminiscent this is of the Sermon on the Mount!) Obey the civil authorities as ordained by God, lead law-abiding lives, pay your taxes. And remember that Christian love is the highest kind of conduct because, hurting nobody, it fulfils the Ten Commandments. Then Paul sounds a *reveille*: 'God's new day is breaking! So off with the deeds of darkness, and put on the moral habits of Christ! If differences arise in your fellowship, the stronger ones should make allowance for the scruples of their weaker brothers. (Evidently in the church at Rome there were differences of opinion about vegetarianism and the keeping of holy days.) No more censorious judging then – we must all appear before the judge of all! (Again, how reminiscent this is of Christ's 'Judge not, that you be not judged.')

'Of course nothing is really unclean, but thinking may make it appear so. Let love then be your law and never count food more important than your Lord did his life. Pursue peace with all men, and better abstain than give offence to a weaker brother.

Christ did not please himself; no more should we. Since he has received you, you should receive each other. And may the God of hope fill you with all joy and peace in believing!' (12.1–15.13).

The sin of man, *but* the grace of God, *therefore* the Christian ethic – such is the gospel as Paul expounded it to his Roman readers.

That Rome in AD 57 (when Paul was writing) needed radical moral cleansing is beyond dispute. 'The sinful city on the seven hills,' men called her. We have only to read Suetonius' 'Lives of the Emperors' to find proof that Paul has not imported too much lamp-black into his picture of the moral evil of the time. Of the great Julius Caesar himself our historian records that he was 'every woman's man and every man's woman'. It is a sobering comment. For all her might and magnificence Rome teemed with wickedness. She might bestride the world like a Colossus: she might spread her conquests from the Euphrates to the Thames; but she could do nothing to cleanse and regenerate the victims of lust and sin with which her realms were filled. Are we in much different spiritual plight today? What a clever creature is twentieth-century man! What mastery over the material world he can claim! Can he not capture the wandering voices of the ether in a tiny transistor, and split the atom to release illimitable sources of energy, and plant his gleaming space-ships in the immensities of God's universe?

Ah, but this is only one side of the medal, and, alas, the other side will hardly bear inspecting. The truth is that modern man, for all his diabolical cleverness, is a tragic figure. He prostitutes his great gifts for the production of atomic bombs which may dissolve the world in nuclear holocaust. He befuddles himself with drink and drugs and under their influence commits crimes of which the lower creation would be ashamed. His great cities abound with thugs and gangsters, and vice, vandalism and violence too often make the headlines of the news.

Nor is the corruption and wickedness confined to the slums and slum-dwellers. It spreads to the highest places in government, as it no less disfigures big business. Many things modern man can do. One thing he cannot do – and that the most needful of all – he cannot. Quite manifestly he cannot save himself.

Is there then no hope for what Frederick the Great called 'the perishing human race' (*die verdammte Rasse*)? 'God forbid!' Paul answers; for it is just here that the gospel of Christ comes in. In it we have God's assurance to sinful man that he has not left him to perish in his sin but is resolved upon his rescue. And what Paul said in AD 57 is as true now as it was then. Still today the gospel remains 'the power of God unto salvation' for every man ready to take him at his living and delivering Word in Christ.

When are 'the wise men of this world' (as Paul would have called them) going to realize that the sickness of our society today is never going to be cured merely by higher education or improved psychological techniques, by economist's blueprint or politician's panacea? At the root of all our malaise lies something they tend to forget – supposing men to be fundamentally good – though the evidence for it lies all around them in the world today.[18] It is what our fathers and forefathers called original sin (sin which is not so much what we do as what we are), the pride and greed and wickedness of men. With this no act of Parliament can cope:

> The heart aye's the part aye
> That makes us right or wrang.[19]

And it is there, within ourselves, as our Lord said (Mark 7.14–23), that the root of the trouble lies. For this 'heart' disease, there is still but one effective remedy, that gospel of God's grace in Christ for sinners which Paul called his dynamic for saving men.

6

Paul as Churchman

It is told of a certain statesman that he said to his colleagues gathered to consider some policy of high importance, 'Gentlemen, you must consult bigger maps.' Don't we Christians need to consult bigger theological maps, especially when we think about the church?

Parochial thinking about it is a fault to which Protestants are specially prone. We equate it with a building – our own place of worship; or with a denomination – our own one of course; or even with a clerical class. ('Here comes the church', we say when the minister comes down the street!)

But the church is far more than a building, or a denomination, or a clerical class. It is the *Ecclēsia*, that is, the new and true people of God, set up by Christ's cross and resurrection and the coming of the Holy Spirit, with a mission which is meant to embrace the world.

This is the burden of Ephesians. It is one of four letters – the others being Colossians, Philemon and Philippians – which Paul wrote, about AD 60–62, from his prison in Rome.[20] Because in our best manuscripts the words 'in Ephesus' are missing, scholars believe that Paul had in mind more than the Christians there, that his letter was meant for all the chief churches in what was then called proconsular Asia. The bearer of the letter, Tychicus (6.21), would reach Ephesus first on his travels – hence the inclusion in some manuscripts of the words 'in Ephesus'. Ephesians, then, is probably a *circular letter*, 'evidently directed to the whole of what might be called Paul's diocese'.[21]

How magnificently it opens! (Read its first chapter for yourself, preferably in the Revised Standard Version or the New English Bible, and not in the Authorized Version, where the inordinately long sentences and abstract phrases are apt to bewilder the reader.)

After Paul's opening address to his readers, he breaks out into a *Te Deum* for all the spiritual blessings which are ours in Christ (1.3–14). Here is Christian doctrine, but doctrine (might one say?) set to music, a great overture to all that is to follow (compare the majestic prologue to John's Gospel). And, as we con its recurring 'in hims' (all referring to Christ), we perceive that all revolves round one central point – God's sovereign will working itself out in Christ and the church to a glorious consummation.

When we fell to discussing God's ways with man in the world, an old Scottish Calvinist woman of our acquaintance used to silence all doubters with the question, 'And do you think He hadn't a plan?' She might have been thinking of Ephesians, which was Calvin's favourite epistle. For the theme of Ephesians is: 'God's plan for the fullness of time to unite all things in Christ, things in heaven and things in earth' (Eph. 1.10 RSV). Earlier, in I Cor. 5.19, Paul had written 'God was in Christ reconciling the world to himself'. In Ephesians he spells out God's plan, and it is seen to embrace not humanity alone but the whole creation.

Of the letter's six chapters the first three provide the doctrine, the second three the ethics following from it. For, as somebody has put it, 'In the New Testament truth is always truth *in order to* goodness.' And the burden of both parts of the letter is the high calling of the church as the society which embodies in history the eternal purpose of God. Let us try to make Paul's doctrine clearer by teasing out the themes of the first three chapters.

1. *Behind this created universe and shaping the course of history is 'one God and Father of all' from whom 'every family in heaven and earth takes its name'.* In his 'beloved' (Christ) he has graciously destined us to be his sons, as for all his creatures he intends community.

But, alas, there is a great rift at the heart of things. Evil, supramundane and mundane, has infected the creation. In the

41

unseen world dwell demonic forces (2.2; 3.10; 6.12), under a master-strategist, which bedevil the course of history and, lodging in men's hearts, turn them into God's rebel subjects. So they disrupt the fair order God designed for his creation. This fatal rift in the world's order only God can repair, and it is his purpose in Christ to subdue all hostile powers and create a final unity in heaven and earth.

2. *God's plan is centred in Christ.* The gospel is the good news of God's 'unveiled secret' (the word 'mystery' in the letter means not an enigma but a long-hidden purpose now made plain in the Christian revelation). This unveiled secret is embodied in Christ who is the integrating centre – the principle of unity – in God's universe.

When 'the time was ripe' (1.10), God put his plan into effect by sending his beloved Son to atone for men's sins, raising him from the dead, and enthroning him in heaven where he now reigns over all potentates and powers (1.20f.). In all this, God's purpose was nothing less than the reconciliation to himself and to one another of all his rebellious creatures.

3. *It is through the church, the body of the risen and regnant Christ, that God's plan is now being realized.*

The forces which make discord in the world Paul sees epitomized in the Law which, like a barrier, separated men from each other and from God. But by his cross Christ has broken down the great 'dividing wall' between Jew and Gentile (2.14).[22] By 'killing the enmity' between them, he has made the two one, and paved the way for a single new humanity. Now, by the Spirit, the living Christ imparts himself through the church which he died to create. Just as he once took to himself a human body for the purpose of his earthly ministry, so now, risen and exalted, he has undergone a larger incarnation. For the church is his body, a spiritual organism energized by Christ, its living head. As a result, the old barriers are going down. Gentiles, once 'far off' from divine grace and 'without hope and God in the world', are now 'fellow citizens with God's people' and members of his household (2.19).

Yet this healing of an ancient division is only the prelude to something still vaster – the movement, under God, of all created beings to an ultimate unity in Christ. When that time comes, there will be one great new humanity, enjoying access, through Christ, in one Spirit, to the Father of all (2.18).

So, in chapters 1–3, St Paul expounds God's plan in Christ, ending with a noble prayer (3.14–19) and doxology.

> Now to him who by the power at work within us is able to do far more abundantly than all that we ask or think, to him be glory in the church and in Christ Jesus to all generations, for ever and ever. Amen.

In Part Two of Ephesians Paul describes the behaviour required of Christians who would 'live up to their high calling' (4.1).

First, *they are to promote the church's unity and growth by means of the various grace-gifts Christ gives for the upbuilding of his body* (4.1–16). The church is one, and seven things make it so: one body, one Spirit, one hope, one Lord, one faith, one baptism, one God and Father of all.

How far the church still falls short of this high calling, and how sadly our unhappy divisions damage its witness to the world, sincere Christians know only too well. Yet, in this twentieth century divided Christendom has begun to heed, in strong earnest, this call to unity; and though there may be 'a long, long trail a-winding' before ecumenical dreams come true, Paul holds out for us a vision of the coming great church; and as we profess and call ourselves Christians who are sick of sectarianism, we must work and pray for the time when there will be 'one church, one faith, one Lord'.

Second: we are to *give up living like pagans* (4.17–5.20), be done with the old lies and lusts, and begin the new life of purity and truth to which God calls us in Christ.

In that hard pagan world of the first century AD this was no easy command to obey. Who will say it has grown easier for Christians today exposed to all the pressures of the permissive society, with its sexual licence, its money-lust, its addiction to drink and drugs? Yet, now as then, Christians are called 'as

43

God's dear children to be like him' (5.1) and to 'walk as children of light' (5.8).

Third, *we are to build Christian homes* (5.21–6.9): homes where a shared reverence for Christ our Lord will create in the whole household – husbands and wives, parents and children, masters and men – that blend of love and respect, forbearance and obedience, discipline and service, which will make the family a miniature of God's great family, the church, which Christ died to create and to sanctify.

Is not this still our Christian duty today? We are all aware how many insidious factors conspire to the break-up of Christian home-life and what Wordsworth called 'pure religion breathing household laws'. So much the more it becomes our duty to keep the holy fire burning on the family altar, to train up our children in the Christian way, and to let the faith, hope and love of the gospel irradiate our hearths and homes.

Fourth: we must *'put on all the armour which God provides'* (6.10–20): the belt of truth, for a breastplate integrity, for our feet the gospel of peace, for a shield faith, for a helmet salvation, for a sword the Spirit-given word of God. Above all, we must keep on praying.

Why should all this spiritual armour be needed? Paul answers in effect: 'Because the church has a real fight on its hands, and that not merely against human adversaries. We are up against superhuman foes – unseen malignant forces and agents from the very headquarters of evil' (6.12).

But (someone will say) does not Paul here betray himself as wholly a man of his time? Time was, and not so very long ago, when enlightened modern men could write off all this as first-century mythology, and dismiss the devil as a discredited bug-bear from man's childhood. Are we so sure nowadays? Two colossal world-wars and their awful aftermaths have made many think again. Have we not seen great civilized nations going berserk like a man possessed of devils and descending to bestial depths of wickedness? Has there not been today an upsurge of interest in Satanism and the black arts? Nay, have not eminent Christian thinkers like Paul Tillich, C. S. Lewis and J. S. Stewart

44

made the dimension of the demonic intellectually respectable? If we still pronounce Paul's language mythological,

> Myth is the language which contains the clue
> To that which is at once both real and true,

and it signals at the existence in the universe of something (or beings) really wild and demonic for whose conquest nothing less than the gospel armour will suffice.

Such is the message of Ephesians for today. Coleridge called the letter 'one of the divinest compositions of man'. Ecumenical theologians like John Mackay of Princeton have seen in it 'the epistle for today'. Before us Paul holds out his 'vision splendid' of the church as the working body of Christ, with a mission to bind the nations in a great brotherhood of worship and of love under the one God and Father of all who has given his Son for the world's saving. To all men cowering behind their ideological iron curtains and living a barbed-wire existence, it holds out its warning: 'Unite – or perish!' And to us who fight under Christ's banner, with no weapons but the weapons of love, it summons: 'Onward, Christian soldiers!'

> On to the end of the road,
> On to the City of God!

7

Paul as Friend

'They say and do not', was Christ's complaint about the Jewish churchmen of his day (Matt. 23.3). It is always good to see a man practising what he preaches. In Ephesians Paul had bidden his readers 'speak the truth in love' (Eph. 4.15). No better example of it could be found than his own letter to his 'dear friend and fellow-worker', Philemon, and the little group of Christians that met in his house. Rightly has it been called a masterpiece of letter-writing. But, first, to the moving human story of the runaway slave called Onesimus.

The scene of the drama is laid first in Colossae, a town lying a hundred miles east of Ephesus in Asia Minor, and the three chief actors in it are Paul, a citizen of Colossae named Philemon, and his slave Onesimus.

When, through Paul's evangelism in Ephesus, the gospel had found its way inland to Colossae, among the first converts had been Philemon and his wife Apphia. They were good Christians, and members of the local congregation used to meet under their roof. But unfortunately one of Philemon's slaves had helped himself to some of his master's money, and absconded. Whither he went on the first stage of his wandering we do not know; but eventually he turned up in Rome, drifting there no doubt as similar persons today might drift to London if they had money to burn. There Providence took a strange but blessed hand in his affairs.

About this time Paul had come to Rome to stand trial as a Christian before Caesar; and one day the door of his prison opened to admit – Onesimus. How he discovered Paul we cannot

46

say; but we may easily imagine him blurting out his tale of shame to the apostle. The sequel was that, under Paul's influence, Onesimus became a Christian and proved himself a great comfort to the apostle. Paul grew very fond of the runaway slave, but he knew that it was his duty, when the opportunity arose, to send Onesimus back to his rightful master. The chance came soon. One day there arrived a messenger from Colossae reporting the outbreak of heresy in the church there and requesting Paul's guidance. So Paul sat down and wrote a letter to the Christians in Colossae – our Epistle to the Colossians – but before he put his pen away, he wrote a little note to Philemon about Onesimus. It is our letter. In it Paul tells Philemon he is sending Onesimus back, asks him to reinstate the slave in his favour, and hints that he would like Philemon to release Onesimus for further Christian service with himself.

Now let us quickly go through the contents of the letter's twenty-five verses.

'Paul, a prisoner of Christ Jesus and our colleague Timothy,' it begins, 'to our dear friend and fellow-worker Philemon, Apphia our sister, Archippus our comrade-in-arms and the congregation in your house. Grace and peace to you from God our Father and the Lord Jesus Christ.'

Then, very tactfully, Paul paves the way for his chief point in writing: 'I thank God always when I mention you in my prayers, for as I learn of your love and loyalty to the Lord Jesus and all God's people, I pray that the sharing of your faith may promote the knowledge of all the good that is ours in Christ. I have had great joy and encouragement from your love, because your action, dear brother, has put new heart into God's people.'

Evidently, some recent act of kindness by Philemon had reached Paul's ears. He is glad to mention it because he is about to say something which will put a severe strain on their friendship. Then, very delicately, he comes to the point:

'Hence, though I would feel quite free to order you to do your duty, I prefer to appeal to you for love's sake. Well then, as Paul the old man, who nowadays is a prisoner for Christ's sake, I appeal to you for my child whose father I have become in prison.'

If these last words must, momentarily, have puzzled Philemon, with the next sentence Paul lets his secret out: 'It is Onesimus I mean.' (Here we may note that the name Onesimus in Greek means useful, and observe what happy play Paul now makes with his name.):

' "Useful" was anything but profitable to you in the past; but today he has become, true to his name, very profitable, both to you and to me. I would fain have kept him here, for in sending him back I feel like parting with my own heart. But I did not want to do anything without your consent.'

'Perhaps (Paul proceeds) this was why you and he were parted for a while, that you might get him back for good, no longer as a mere slave but as something more – a dear brother, dear indeed to me but how much more to you, both as a man and as a Christian.'

Then comes Paul's final appeal: 'You count me a partner in the faith? Then welcome Onesimus as you would me. Ah, but maybe you are still remembering the money he stole? Well, put it down to my account. Here is my own IOU for the amount: I PAUL WILL REPAY, SIGNED WITH MY OWN HAND, PAUL. Come, brother, let me get some use from you in the Lord. I write, confident that you will obey and do even more than I ask.'

With a request to get a room ready for him, since he hopes to be freed, Paul sends greetings from his friends, (John Mark and 'the beloved physician', Luke, among them) and ends with a benediction.

The fact that this tiny semi-private letter of Paul's has been preserved is surely evidence that Paul's plea for Onesimus did not fail. But we may go further. In verse 20 of the letter Paul writes: 'Yes, brother, I want some benefit (or use) from you in the Lord.' Now Paul's Greek verb here, *onaimen*, is the verbal form of Onesimus. The apostle is punning on his name. He is saying, 'Let me make a profit from you', and his meaning is much clearer if Onesimus himself is the profit he is after! Similarly, in the next verse, Paul says, 'I know you will do even more than I say.' If the apostle has not explicitly said that he wants Onesimus not only reinstated in his master's favour but returned to himself for active service, he has thrown out a pretty broad hint! Did Philemon take it? Did Onesimus later become a comrade-in-arms of St Paul and, eventually, a notable Christian in his own right? There is evidence that he did. Forty years later, about AD 110, Ignatius, the bishop of Antioch, writing to the Christians in Ephesus, refers three times to their bishop, one Onesimus, whom he calls 'a man of inexpressible love' (Ignatius, *To the Ephesians* 1.3). Many scholars believe that Ignatius is referring to the subject of Paul's letter to Philemon. Onesimus had made good.

Rightly has Paul's little letter been called 'the most gentlemanly letter ever written', by the famous 'Rabbi' Duncan of New College, Edinburgh, as the story behind it has been named 'an idyll of grace'. But does it not also reveal its writer as a true follower of him who, while he walked this earth, was called 'the friend of sinners'?

8

Paul as Saint

That deeply spiritual Catholic layman, Baron von Hügel, being asked what qualities his church looked for in those she canonized as saints, said there were four: 'Loyalty to the faith, heroism in time of testing, the power to do what ordinarily would seem humanly impossible, and radiance amid the stress and strain of life.'

It is in Philippians that Paul most clearly qualifies on the last of these criteria. Written from his Roman prison in the early sixties,[23] and possibly his 'swan song', the letter's primary purpose is to say thank you for a gift from his congregation in Philippi (a leading city of Macedonia, in northern Greece) conveyed to him by the hand of one of their members named Epaphroditus.

Dear Christians in Philippi,' Paul begins, 'my memories of you are a continual joy to me, as I pray that you are growing in love and knowledge and insight. My imprisonment here has really turned out to be a blessing in disguise since, one way or another, it has led to more preaching of Christ; and for this I rejoice. What the future holds is uncertain. For myself, I am torn in two directions. If it holds death, I shall go and be with my Lord, which would be best for me. Yet, for your sake, it is probably better that I should stay on in the body. Whatever happens, I want you to stand firm for the Gospel of Christ against all your enemies(1).

'Above all, live together in harmony, and be humble – like Christ himself who, though he was in God's form, became servant upon earth and died upon a cross, so that God highly exalted him, bestowing on him the name above all names. So work out your own salvation – with God's help – by your blameless lives shine out like stars in a dark world, and on the Day of Judgment I shall have cause to be proud of you. With this letter I am sending back Epaphroditus who has been dangerously ill, and soon I hope to send the trusty Timothy who in the service of the gospel has worked with me like a son under his father. God willing, I shall myself be coming before long(2).

'Be on your guard against those curs, those would-be mutilators of your bodies (Jewish Christians insisting on circumcision). Once, I might have boasted myself a better Jew than any of them, but all my Jewish privileges and rights I gladly sacrificed when through faith in Christ I found peace with God and had my whole life changed. Not that I consider myself now "perfect"; but, like a runner, I press on towards the goal for the prize, which is God's call to life above, in Christ Jesus.

'To be a mature Christian is my aim. Make it yours also. And have no truck with those libertines whose only god is their belly. Remember that we are citizens of heaven and await a Saviour who will change our present lowly bodies into glorious ones, like his own(3).

'Please help these two quarrelling women in the congregation to be friends again: they once shared my struggles for the Gospel's sake, along with Clement and others whose names are in the book of life.

'Finally, all joy be yours; have no anxiety; keep saying your prayers; and wherever you find virtue and merit among your pagan neighbours, take it into your account.

'I was overjoyed by your practical remembrance of me. Long experience has taught me to cope with all the ups and downs of life, and in union with Christ I am able for anything. Yet, thank you for your gift, not the first you have sent me. All God's people here send their greetings, especially those belonging to the imperial establishment.

'The grace of the Lord Jesus Christ be with your spirit'(4).

'The sum of the letter,' said the old German commentator Johannes Bengel, 'is: "I rejoice, and you must also rejoice." ' No

51

fewer than sixteen times do the words 'joy' and 'rejoice' occur in Philippians, which is an average of four 'joys' per chapter. 'My joy and crown', Paul proudly calls his converts. If they will but agree among themselves, as Christians should, they will 'complete his joy'. And not once but thrice he bids them 'rejoice in the Lord!' To all long-faced and lugubrious Christians, Philippians, 'the epistle radiant with joy', remains a perpetual rebuke. By the last of Von Hügel's tests Paul is certainly a saint.

Now for his first one: 'loyalty to the faith'. The gospel which Paul proclaimed was the gospel which all the apostles proclaimed (see I Cor. 15.1–11) and they libel the apostle who say otherwise. No perverter of the gospel, he nonetheless grasped the magnitude of the redemption God had wrought in Christ better than any other.

When he speaks as he sometimes does (e.g. Rom. 2.16; Gal. 2.2) of 'my gospel', or 'the gospel which I preach', it is the common apostolic gospel stamped with his own special experience and bearing his own emphases and insights. Nonetheless, the Christ who is its living centre is the same Christ whom Peter and the other apostles confessed as Lord and Son of God. Let none question Paul's fidelity to the gospel or deny his right to say, as he did near the end of his life, 'I have kept the faith' (II Tim. 4.7).

After 'loyalty to the faith' comes 'heroism in time of testing'. Should anyone doubt Paul's title to this quality, let him read Luke's account of the great storm which befell the ship taking the apostle to Rome (Acts 27). At every crisis in the tempestuous voyage it is Paul who puts heart of courage into the ship's company. Or let him turn to II Cor. 11.24–28. Stung into reply by the slanders of his enemies, Paul lists the hardships he has undergone as an ambassador for Christ. 'Many a time,' he writes, 'I have been face to face with death. Five times the Jews gave me thirty-nine strokes with the lash. Thrice I was beaten with Roman rods. Three times I was shipwrecked. For twenty-four hours I was adrift in the open sea.' Then he recalls dangers from rivers, from robbers, from false friends, all the times he had gone without sleep or food, suffering cold and exposure, to which external tribulations there fell to be added his daily weight of 'worry about all his churches'. Set beside all this, how cosy and uncosting seems most of our Christian witness today! What incomparable fortitude was Paul's for the gospel's sake! 'I reckon fortitude's the biggest thing a man can have,' says Peter Pienaar in Buchan's *Mr Standfast*, 'just to go on when there's no heart or guts left in you.' Then, naming two men who had shown it, he ended, 'But the head man at the job was the apostle Paul.'

Precisely so: if resolute courage to keep going on in face of fearful odds is one test of sainthood, Paul passes with flying colours.

The last of Von Hügel's 'tests' was 'the power to do what ordinarily would seem humanly impossible'. What in the first century AD might have been so described? Would it not have been the conquest of the Roman empire for Christ? Yet something very like this was the goal Paul set himself, and how nearly he had attained it before he was martyred!

'There is something astounding in the magnitude of the task Paul set himself,' wrote Dean Inge, 'and in his enormous success. By his labours the future history of the world for two thousand years, and perhaps for all time, was determined.'[24] With none of our modern means of swift and easy travel, or of communications, this dynamic little man tramped all over Asia and a good deal of Europe, making it his ambition to bring the gospel to 'places where the very name of Christ has not been heard' (Rom. 15.20). By AD 57 he had completed his preaching of the gospel from Jerusalem in the east to Illyricum (Yugoslavia) in the west (Rom. 15.19). And now, God willing, he was planning to proclaim it in the world's metropolis before going on to Spain (Rom. 15.28).

Reach Rome he did, and from his prison there continued to bear his witness, even among those 'who belong to the imperial establishment' (Phil. 4.21). Nor is it impossible that he set foot on Spanish soil, for Clement of Rome, writing about AD 95, says that before Paul went to glory, he 'reached the limit of the west' (which sounds like Gibraltar). And all this he accomplished in a body racked by sharp physical pain (II Cor. 12.7). If this is not to 'do what ordinarily would seem humanly impossible', what else is it?

Yet, as Paul is indubitably a saint, he is none of your ethereal ones wearing luminous halos and invested with dubious legends. To this type Paul refuses to conform – even in his physical appearance; for, according to the second-century *Acts of Paul and Thekla*, 'he was short and bald, with bandy legs, a hooked nose, and beetling brows': a description so unflattering that it invites belief.

Had Paul been some shadowy moral paragon, he would never, down nineteen centuries, have been so hated by a few or been so 'loved this side idolatry' by a multitude who have found in him the most heroic figure in the early church and the supreme interpreter of the fact of Christ.

Moreover, though dead and 'gone to be with Christ' these nineteen centuries, he is yet posthumously alive, his words still, as Martin Luther said, 'hands and feet to carry a man away'.

'The style,' said Buffon, 'is the man', and the person who emerges from Paul's letters is a highly-strung man, writing sometimes with his nerves in a kind of blaze, yet possessing a warm heart, a sanctified common sense, and a powerful mind which, when it rises to the height of its great theme, can utter itself in unforgettable Christian speech.

Normally tender, affectionate and quick to 'speak the truth in love', he can yet, when he sees the truth of the gospel being compromised, blaze out in righteous indignation.

A born leader of men, something of a mystic (see II Cor. 12.1ff.) and yet a great man of action, he has an unshakable conviction of the reality of the unseen world, and of his own choice by God to play a supreme part in spreading the gospel of Christ to the whole world.

Above all, his devotion to his Lord and Saviour is complete. 'Life', he says simply, 'means Christ to me' (Phil. 1.21, Moffatt).

And Paul, being dead and gone to glory long ago, yet speaks to us today, if only we will hear him. Of course, often in his letters he shows himself as a man of his time addressing his contemporaries. But, as Karl Barth said, as apostle of Christ and the kingdom, he can yet speak to all men of every age. For, if we rightly understand ourselves and our human predicament, our problems are the problems of Paul, and if we are enlightened by the brightness of Paul's answers, those answers must be ours too.

Some of us long to see the church today returning to the gospel of the fifth evangelist. What we have in mind is no uncritical fundamentalism – there is no real future in this – but a gospel built on a Pauline foundation – a gospel which takes seriously the sinfulness of sin, proclaims God's free grace to sinners, and has at its heart a commanding Christ and a redeeming cross: a gospel which expounds these truths in modern ways, and looks to the work of the Holy Spirit to make them real in men's lives today. (Here, without endorsing all their doctrines, we may learn from our latter-day Pentecostals.)

As a matter of history, down the centuries revival in the church has not seldom begun with the rediscovery of the gospel according to St Paul – think of Augustine, Luther, Wesley and Barth, to name only the great names. Wherefore, for the renewing of the church of Christ today, we make bold to say: 'Back to that gospel which is the power of God unto salvation to everyone that believeth.'

9

'Whatsoever things are true'

High among St Paul's memorable sentences stands that in his letter to the Philippians which begins, 'Whatsoever things are true' and ends with the injunction 'think on these things' (Phil. 4.8).

The words are undoubtedly Paul's; but when you come to examine them, they are, to say the least, unusual in Paul. Here is a paraphrase of them:

'All that rings true (*alethē*), all that commands reverence (*semna*), all that makes for right (*dikaia*), all that is pure (*hagna*), all that is attractive (*prosphilē*), all that is high-toned (*euphēma*): virtue (*aretē*) and merit (*epainos*), wherever virtue and merit are found, take them into your account (*logizesthe*).'

This is not Paul's Christian ethic. Not a word about the imitation of Christ, not a reference to that Christian love (*agapē*) of which he had sung so lyrically in I Cor. 13. Instead, we find eight Greek words, three of which (*prosphilē, euphēma*, and *aretē*) are not found elsewhere in his letters and one (*semna*) which occurs only in the Pastoral Epistles. The whole verse in fact suggests not Christian but pagan ideals. It extols just those moral values which you might have found commended in any contemporary Greek manual of ethics. Why then this unexpected praise by Paul of pagan moral excellences?

The passage was probably written in answer to a question from his converts in Philippi.[25] What attitude (they had asked) ought we to adopt to what is good in the heathen society around us?

Mark the magnanimity of the apostle's answer. Some three centuries later St Augustine was to dismiss the virtues of the pagans as 'brilliant vices'. Far other is Paul's reply: 'Truth is truth,' he says in effect, 'virtue is virtue wherever found; merit is merit, whoever manifests it. And you must take these things into your reckoning.'

Today, in what has been called 'the post-Christian age', paganism – or perhaps the 'in' word is secularism – begins very often just outside our own church doors. Many of our neighbours are not unlike Paul's Gentiles, 'without hope or God in the world' (Eph. 2.12). In such a situation the Christian preacher is often tempted to denounce the sins and vices of this generation root and branch. Yet among these so-called pagans, do we not often, and quite unexpectedly, come on real goodness, rare kindness, and a sincere concern for truth and justice?

When we encounter such virtues, Paul tells us, we ought to recognize them for what they are and take them into our account.

But how are we to explain 'the goodness of the godless', as it has been called?

Once in the gospels (Mark 10.17–22) a rich young man addressed Jesus as 'Good Master'. Jesus' reply was, 'Why do you call me good? No one is good but God alone.' This was not a disclaimer by Jesus of his own goodness. The questioner's idea of goodness was clearly that of a goodness which was *man*'s achievement. Jesus at once directs his attention away from himself to God who is the source of all goodness (see James 1.17, 'Every good endowment and every perfect gift is from above'). Thus the goodness of the men we call godless is from above, 'God being with them though they know it not.'

The moral for us Christians is obvious. When we come on such goodness in men or women who for one reason or another are not believers, let us 'take it into our account' and give thanks to God the great giver.

10

By Faith or by Works?

Romans 3.28: A man is justified by *faith* apart from works of the law.

James 2.24: A man is justified by *works*, and not by faith alone.

Here are two apparently contradictory statements on a matter of much importance. St Paul says: 'Justification (i.e. acceptance with God) is by faith.' St James says: 'Justification is by works, and not faith only.' It sounds as if James were correcting Paul, or some widely prevalent view of his teaching. Are, then, these two apostles at odds with each other on the question of how a man is to get right with God?

Practically all Paul's teaching on the subject is to be found in Romans, Galatians and the third chapter of Philippians. This is very significant. 'Justification by faith' appears in his letters when he is confronting Jewish legalism in the church.

On the problem we are discussing it would appear that not a few early Christians sided with St James. Acceptance with God, they held, comes by doing the works of the Law, and not by faith alone. On one point Paul did not disagree: 'Without righteousness – rightness with holy God – there is no fellowship with him, no salvation.' It was when the question arose, 'How does a man get right with God?', that Paul and the Jewish Christians parted company. They said, 'Only the man who fulfils the Law can hope for acceptance with God.'

Now before his conversion this had been Paul's view also. But after he had met the risen Christ on the Damascus Road, it was so no longer. In that memorable hour when (to use his own verb) he had been 'arrested by Christ' (Phil. 3.12), it was revealed to him that his very zeal for the Law had involved him in sin of the most grievous kind – had made him a persecutor of Jesus, God's Messiah, who had died for sinners (I Cor. 15.3) and was now very much alive. Henceforward Paul was convinced that rightness with God was not to be found that way. Now he said, 'No human being can be justified in the sight of God for having kept the Law: Law brings only consciousness of sin' (Rom. 3.20 NEB).

So Paul's whole view of salvation was radically changed. By faith and not by works was the way to acceptance with God. Taking a sentence from the prophet Habakkuk (Hab. 2.4), he gave it a new meaning: 'He who through faith is righteous shall live' – shall be saved (Rom. 1.17).[26]

But does this not mean that faith itself is a work, an achievement, for which God accepts a sinful man? Achievement it is, but the achievement not of the sinner but of Christ and the cross. Faith lays hold of Christ's finished work – his atoning death – and presents it to God saying, 'I believe that Christ died, by your appointing, for my sins.' Thus the way to acceptance with God is not by works of the law but by trust in the living crucified.

Sola fide, 'by faith alone', this then was Paul's first great conviction. His second was like unto it: *sola gratia*, by grace alone. We men are sinners who cannot save ourselves. All depends on God and what he does. What then? When we put our faith in his Christ, God, of his sheer grace – his unmerited love to sinners – puts us right with himself, forgive us, and sets our feet on 'the way everlasting'. As Thomas Chalmers, centuries later, was to say in his great simplicity, 'What could I do if God did not justify the ungodly?'

Is, then, justification by faith a peculiarly Pauline doctrine, arising perhaps out of his own religious experience? On the contrary, as Gal. 2.11–16 shows. There Paul tells us that Peter, in spite of his vacillation at Antioch, really took the same view. 'You and I,' said Paul, 'are Jews by birth, not Gentiles. But we know that no man is ever justified by doing what the Law demands, but only through faith in Christ Jesus' (Gal. 2.15f. NEB).

But this is not all. Justification by faith is something that goes back to their common Lord and his teaching. If Paul in his day had to contend with Jewish legalists in the church, earlier Jesus himself had been fighting the same good fight in his controversy with the Pharisees.

Both Jesus and Paul agree that no one is so far from God as the self-righteous man. Did not Jesus say in his first beatitude, 'How blest (divinely happy) are those who know their need of God!' (Matt. 5.3 NEB). Did he not also say, 'I came not to call the righteous (i.e. those sure of their own righteousness, "the unco' guid", as Burns was to name them) but sinners' (Mark 2.16)? Nay more, does he not in his parables teach justification by faith? Is not his parable of the gracious father and his ne'er-do-well son a perfect picture of it? Does not his story about the good employer (Matt. 20.1–15) teach the same lesson: 'God treats sinners as that kind employer treated those unemployed men.' And does not the same truth ring out in the parable of the Pharisee and the publican? 'This man,' says Jesus of the penitent tax-collector, 'went down to his house justified (*dedikaiōmenos*, Paul's very word) rather than the other (the Pharisee who reminded God of all his goods works)?' In fine, Paul's doctrine of justification by faith is but the development of what Jesus had taught in his holy warfare with the self-righteous Pharisees.

How, then, is the apparent difference of opinion between St Paul and St James to be explained?

A wise judge once said that most of the disputes in the world would be well on their way to settlement if only the disputants would begin by defining their terms.

The terms here are three: faith, works and justification. Let us observe how differently the two apostles use them.

If you study James 2.14–26, you discover that for James faith means the intellectual acceptance of monotheism – belief in one God (2.9). For Paul, however, faith means believing that God

60

gave Christ to die for our sins and raised him for our justification (Rom. 4.24f.).

Next, for James works means what we would call practical Christianity – feeding the hungry and clothing the naked (James 2.14–17). For Paul works mean keeping the commandments, circumcision, and all the dictates of the Torah.

Finally, James and Paul use the verb justify differently. In grammar, the pundits dist nguish between analytical and synthetic propositions. When James asks, 'Was not Abraham our father justified by his works?' (James 2.21), he is using the verb *analytically*. God (he means) recognized and rewarded Abraham's existing righteousness. But when Paul talks of 'God justifying the ungodly' (Rom. 4.5), he uses the verb *synthetically*. That is to say, in acting as he does, God adds something – in fact, bestows righteousness on the sinner, sets him right with himself, forgives him, as the father did his prodigal son in the parable.

Formally, then, Rom. 3.28 and James 2.24 contradict each other. In fact, the difference between Paul and James is small. And this becomes clear when we remember the different areas of conflict in which the two men were engaged.

What Paul is combating is the Jewish doctrine of meritorious works. To this the apostle opposes his great watchword: 'By faith alone, by grace alone.' So, as we have seen, had his Lord done before him (Matt. 5.3; Luke 18.14). *Per contra*, what James is combating is a dead orthodoxy. Faith without practical Christianity is, he rightly says, a lifeless thing (2.17). And had not Jesus himself said much the same thing in his Sermon on the Mount (Matt. 7.21: 'Not everyone who calls me "Lord, Lord" will enter the kingdom of heaven, but only those who do the will of my heavenly Father', NEB)? Paul then repeats the first beatitude, James the closing verses of the sermon on the mount. We therefore conclude that James has a right to stand after Paul, since his message can only be understood when Paul's has been understood.

Martin Luther dismissed the Epistle of James as 'a right strawy epistle with no tang of the gospel about it'. We can understand why, in his controversy with Rome about the nature of Christian

61

salvation, he did so. Nonetheless, he did James less than justice. His epistle, pithy, prophetic and practical, abides as the needful corrective for those who forget Paul's teaching that true Christian faith is ever active in love (Gal. 5.6) and that God means such faith to issue in good works (Eph. 2.10).

Paul and James have different ways of putting things, as they lay the emphasis in different places; but there is no fundamental disagreement between them. For James would have agreed with Paul that what matters is 'faith working through love', and Paul would have agreed with James that 'faith without works is dead'; and both would have agreed that the first thing to do with faith is to *live* by it.[27]

PART TWO

11

The New Look on St John

How 'the whirligig of time brings in his revenges' and overturns the higher critics' 'orthodoxies' may be seen from the studies in John's Gospel during the last thirty years.[28]

Some seventy years ago a book on the Fourth Gospel by E. F. Scott, then a young Scottish minister (later to become a distinguished American professor), startled many readers brought up on the conservative views of Bishop Westcott. What Scott had done was to introduce British readers to views of the Gospel widely accepted then by German scholars.

To show how much water has flowed under the scholars' bridges in the interval, let us recall the main positions then held by the Germans.

First, the Fourth Evangelist knew and used the synoptic gospels.

Second, his background was not that of the events he recorded. Far from Palestine, in Ephesus, and in the second century he was reinterpreting Christianity for Hellenistic readers.

Third, the evangelist was essentially a witness to the Christ of Christian faith rather than to the historical Jesus.

Fourth, his Gospel was the 'end term' in the theological evolution of the New Testament.

Fifth, the evangelist was not an apostle or a contemporary of Jesus.

The effect of these five judgments was to set John (whoever he was) at one or more removes from the events he records and to minimize the worth of his testimony to the historical Jesus.

Per contra, the effect of much recent study of the gospel – and it is mostly British, not German – has been to cast doubt on most of these judgments and to give us a new appreciation of the historical value of what Clement of Alexandria called 'the spiritual gospel'.

To begin with, a majority of scholars, even in Germany, now deny that John knew the synoptic gospels.[29]

What is the importance of this critical *volte face*? This: if St John is independent of the synoptic gospels, then he is, potentially at least, as near to the source of gospel truth as the synoptists – or their sources (Mark, Q, M and L).

Second, seventy years ago critics like E. F. Scott set the background of the Fourth Gospel among the Hellenists or the Gnostics of the second century. Now the discovery of the Dead Sea Scrolls has shown there is no need, for basic background, to go beyond southern Palestine in the years between the crucifixion and the fall of Jerusalem.

Third, these two considerations – that John is an independent authority for the story of Jesus, and that his basic background is the Palestine of AD 30–70 – have inevitably modified the critics' third opinion that John is not a reliable witness to the Jesus of history. Of course he is a witness to the Christ of faith; but so also are Mark and the other two evangelists. What distinguishes the new look on John's Gospel is a fresh readiness to recognize that in John's tradition we may be as near, and sometimes nearer, than they are.

Fourth, according to the older radical critics, John represented the end term, or final stage, in the theological evolution of the New Testament.

Now no New Testament scholar doubts that St John was a mature Christian thinker. But does matureness necessarily mean lateness? Yes, said these critics, John's theology, owing much to Paul, is the spiritual crown and completion of New Testament thinking about Christ.

But is the theory of evolution, borrowed from the natural world, a safe guide in matters spiritual? Modern scholars doubt it. At any rate, they not only deny John's debt to Paul – fancy a disciple of Paul who does not describe Christ as the second Adam or use the verb 'justify' – but they hold that John is 'a figure with his own originality'.[30]

Finally, a word on the connection between the Fourth Gospel and the apostle John.

In 1880, Westcott, after citing the strong testimony of Irenaeus to the gospel's apostolic authorship, went on to argue that the author was (a) a Jew, (b) a Jew of Palestine, (c) an eye-witness, (d) an apostle, and (e) the apostle John.

Nowadays Johannine neo-conservatives (if we may so call them) like Dr John Robinson aim rather to vindicate the earliness and trustworthiness of John's testimony to Jesus.[31] The gospel claims to depend on eye-witness evidence (John 1.14; 19.35; cf. 18.1f;), and what they seek to do is to trace back the gospel's historical tradition to the earliest days, not through the memory of one old man but through the ongoing life of the Christian community at Ephesus. The result is to give us new confidence in the gospel as a historical source, as may be seen in Raymond Brown's admirable Anchor Bible Company on the gospel.[32]

Now let us deploy some of the evidence supporting the new look on John's Gospel.

First, scholars from C. F. Burney to Matthew Black have shown that John's Greek reveals in many places – particularly the sayings of Jesus – an unmistakable Aramaic accent.

This is not a matter of single words only, e.g. Cephas and Gabbatha; it extends into syntax. John, for example, favours *parataxis*, the setting side by side of complete sentences with main verbs and connected by *kai*, instead of using, as a Greek would, subordinate clauses (e.g. John 9.6f.). This is Aramaic rather than Greek style. So is his liking for *asyndeton*, the omission of connecting particles, which is un-Greek. Another is his odd use of *hina* suggesting an underlying Aramaic *de* (e.g. John 16.2). A fourth is his use of the *redundant pronoun* (e.g. John 1.27: 'of whom I am not worthy to untie the sandal thong *of him*'). But the search for Aramaic influence becomes really interesting when we find not only many examples of that poetical parallelism, or 'rhyming of thoughts', which characterizes Jesus' teaching in, say, the Sermon on the Mount, but even complete strophes with assonance and word play. The conclusion to be drawn from all this is not that the Fourth Gospel is a straight translation from an Aramaic original but that John's Gospel is the work of an Aramaic-speaking writer who used Greek as his second language.

Question: How came an evangelist who composed his gospel in Ephesus to write Greek with an Aramaic accent?

Now let us pass to John's *topography*. Matthew Arnold once opined: 'When John wants a name for a locality, he takes the first village that comes into his remembrance without troubling whether it suits or no.' If John's geography is as happy-go-lucky as Arnold thought, the link we have begun to forge with Palestine will have been seriously weakened. But what in fact do modern archaeologists like Albright say? They tell us that at place after place their investigations have confirmed the accuracy of John's topography. Enough here to say that 'Aenon near Salim' (John 3.23), the Pool of Bethesda (John 5.2), Sychar (John 4.5) and Gabbatha (John 19.13) – the four place names which caused most difficulty – have been identified with virtual certainty. Moreover, most of the places mentioned only in the Fourth Gospel belong to southern Palestine, while Galilean place-names common in the synoptic gospels are not found. This strongly suggests that the Fourth Evangelist (or some informant of his) had a personal interest in that area.[33]

So to the question of *background*. Last century Bishop Lightfoot described the Fourth Gospel as 'perhaps the most Hebraic book in the New Testament'. The discovery of the Dead Sea Scrolls has done much to vindicate his judgment. Down at Qumran, on the north-western shore of the Dead Sea, lived Jews who spoke and thought in the idioms which we have been wont to label 'Johannine' and which for long were pronounced Gnostic and Greek.

You cannot read far in the *Manual of Discipline* until you light on the very un-Greek phrase 'do the truth' (John 3.21). A little later an allusion to him who 'looks at the light of life' will recall Jesus' claim in John 8.12. Further on, the *Manual's* words about creation will ring a Johannine bell in the memory:

By his knowledge everything has been brought into being,
And everything that is, he established by his purpose,
And apart from him nothing is done (cf. John 1.2f.).

Even more important, however, than such echoes of John's vocabulary are the repeatedly contrasted themes – light and darkness, truth and error, life and death – which sound a kind of counterpoint in both John and the Scrolls. Now this dualism in the Qumran documents is of the same sort as John's, and it is not metaphysical (as in Gnosticism), but ethical and eschatological. When alongside this dualism we come on phrases like 'the spirit of truth' and 'eternal life', the verdict of Millar Burrows is justified: 'The Scrolls show us that we do not need to look outside Palestinian Judaism for the soil in which the Johannine theology grew.'[34]

These three approaches, converging as they do on Palestine, strongly suggest that we need to revise our opinion of St John's Gospel as history. Now it is here that the importance of John's independence becomes evident. For, if he did not draw on the synoptics but had traditions of his own, he is potentially, at various points, as good a witness to the Jesus of history as they are, and sometimes better. But how to exploit the possibilities of this new view of John?

In 1958 J. E. Davey, in his *The Jesus of St John*, argued that 'the nucleus of the picture of Jesus and his teaching in St John is fact, not fiction'. In 1960 came A. J. B. Higgins's suggestive *The Historicity of St John*; and in the same year the present writer attacked the problem on the principle of 'intrinsic probability'.[35] The argument was that, if something in John makes obvious sense of what is inexplicit in the synoptics, that 'something' has a fair claim to historicity. Thus, it is to John that we owe the information: 1. that some of Jesus' disciples had previously followed the Baptist (John 1.35); 2. that Jesus exercised a preliminary Judaean ministry, concurrent with the Baptist's, before his Galilean ministry began (John 3.22ff); 3. that at the time of the feeding of the five thousand messianic excitement had reached so dangerous a pitch that a 'revolt in the desert' against hated Rome seemed imminent (John 6.15); and 4. that there was a later ministry in Judaea, with a three months' campaign in Jerusalem, between Jesus' departure from Galilee and the Passover at which he was crucified (John 7–11). The truth of these four statements would now be generally conceded. But, if the gains of the new approach were to be properly harvested, a thorough examination of the whole question was obviously needed. It came in 1963 with C. H. Dodd's *Historical Tradition in the Fourth Gospel*.

His book, a piece of consummate scholarship, fell into two parts: a study of the narratives in John: and an investigation of the Johannine sayings of Jesus.

In Part I Dodd shows that John's passion story rests back on a primitive tradition common to all the evangelists but in the Fourth Gospel representing a third development alongside the passion stories in Mark and Luke. Formulated in Palestine before AD 66 (when the war with Rome broke out), this tradition merits high historical respect. Likewise, earlier narratives in the gospel, e.g. the healings at Bethesda and Siloam, are shown to have been drawn by John from sources of his own.

To this pre-Johannine tradition belong also John's place-names (already discussed) and its 'itinerary fragments' (e.g. John 3.22f).

When, in Part II, Dodd applies form criticism to the sayings of Jesus, he uncovers five pericopes like those in the synoptics; fifteen 'Words of the Lord' reminiscent of those in the synoptics but clearly independent: and eight short parables, as well as sequences of sayings like those in the synoptic tradition.

He concludes that John's tradition about Jesus has its roots in an Aramaic one originating in Palestine between AD 30 and 66, a tradition with which all concerned with the historical Jesus must make serious reckoning.

Enough has been said to show how much good history underlies John's Gospel. The question poses itself: how did the Fourth Evangelist, writing in distant Ephesus, come by it? One thing is certain. His links with Palestine are far stronger than E. F. Scott and continental scholars ever dreamed seventy years ago. Here is a man whose mother-tongue was Aramaic, who knew Jerusalem and Judaea at least as well as the present writer knows Ayr and the land of Burns, whose religious thinking is deeply Jewish, and who had access to some excellent information about Jesus. Yet he wrote in far-off Ephesus. Who was 'John'?

In view of Irenaeus' impressive testimony that the apostle John worked and died in Ephesus and the kind of evidence we have been reviewing,[36] why should it be thought incredible that John the apostle, 'the beloved disciple', stands behind the gospel, that his testimony is embodied in it, and that in this sense he can be called its 'author' (cf. Isaiah in the Old Testament)? On the other hand, various features in the gospel suggest that the actual writer was not the apostle but some close disciple of his.[37]

Now we know that in the third quarter of the first century many Palestinians emigrated to Ephesus and Asia Minor before the fall of Jerusalem.[38] The evidence we have been studying would make good sense if among those emigrants was a close disciple who, after living in Palestine through the first half of the century, joined the apostle John in Ephesus and, after his death, compiled 'the Gospel according to St John'. That this disciple was 'the Elder' to whom we owe the epistles seems reasonably certain. He may have been 'the Elder John' mentioned by Papias. What we have in the Fourth Gospel might therefore be called 'the Gospel of John the Elder according to John the Apostle'.

We are wont to call it 'the Fourth Gospel'. But is it chronologically so? Are we sure it is later than Matthew? John's peculiar phraseology can no longer be made an argument for a late date – thanks to the discovery of the Scrolls. The finding of the Rylands Fragment of John's Gospel in Egypt convinced even Bultmann that the Gospel could not be later than AD 100. The general agreement that John did not know the synoptics means that we need no longer date it ten or more years after them. It may have been written as early as AD 75.[39] But perhaps more important than the new tendency to date the gospel earlier is the proof that the historical tradition embodied in the gospel is Palestinian and belongs to the first generation of Christianity.

All we have been saying about the 'new look' on John's Gospel has made for a *rapprochement* between it and the first three gospels. How different was the situation fifty years ago! Then it had become almost an axiom with scholars that you went to the synoptics for the Jesus of history, and to the Fourth Gospel for the Christ of faith. That assumption has long since broken down, so that the continued isolation of John can no longer be defended.

Yet if we can no longer justify the sharp line-up of the Fourth Gospel against the first three, this is not to say that the difference between them is an illusion. A difference remains, but it is one not of *kind* but of *degree* – a difference in dimension and depth.

This is the position that has always been taken by the best Anglican scholars, from Westcott to William Temple. The words which Browning set on the lips of the dying evangelist in *A Death in the Desert* sum it up:

What first were guessed as points I now knew stars
And named them in the Gospel I have writ.

John's Gospel enables us to see the Christ of the synoptic gospels in depth.

To illustrate the new rapprochement between the Fourth Gospel and the synoptics, let us take two examples.

First, it would not be hard to show that in the matter of miracles the difference is really one of terminology rather than of thought. At first sight John's 'signs' (*sēmeia*) seem very different from the 'mighty works' (*dynameis*) of the synoptics. St John is clearly at pains to bring out the christological overtones of the miracles. Yet he is not importing into the record something not originally there. Even in the synoptics the 'mighty works' are messianic signs – for those who have eyes to see. For evidence we need look no further than Jesus' reply to the Baptist's question from prison. That reply conflates the messianic prophecies about the Day of the Lord in Isa. 35 and 61. For Jesus, his miracles were evidence or signs of the dawning reign of God. Their significance is not that they *prove* him the divine Son of God, but that they are the acts of the Messiah (cf. Matt. 11.2, *ta erga tou Christou*, 'the works of the Messiah'). John but underlines what is implied in the synoptic miracles, that in Jesus' 'mighty works' men are confronted by the presence of God in his saving power. There is no real difference between the synoptic Christ who says, 'If I(*ego*) by the finger of God cast out devils, then is the kingdom of God come upon you' (Luke 11.20) and the Johannine Christ who declares, 'The Father who dwells in me does his works' (John 14.10), since in the synoptic gospels 'the king in the kingdom is a father'.

Second, you may argue that the five sayings about the Paraclete in John 14.16 – though they come to John through independent tradition – simply spell out in fuller and richer language the teaching of Jesus in the synoptics about the Father's gift of the Holy Spirit who would be the disciples' advocate, or helper, in the days beyond the cross (Matt. 10.20; Mark 13.11; Luke 12.12; 24.49).

Nevertheless, there are two major issues – eschatology and christology – which are commonly taken as evidence of the gulf between John and the synoptics. Can we really maintain that in these areas what John has done is to see through to its depth what is implicit in the synoptics?

Take eschatology first. In the synoptics, as Streeter showed years ago,[40] there is a growing tendency to heighten the apocalyptic element in Jesus' teaching, with St Matthew 'the chief of sinners' in this respect. *Per contra*, what we find in John is a strong stress on realized eschatology, without, however, complete exclusion of the future note.

Formerly, when everybody assumed that John depended on the synoptics, the suggestion lay to hand that he deliberately toned down this apocalyptic heightening. Now that John is seen to be independent, we may hold that he preserves a tradition of Jesus' teaching which has not been apocalypticized and more truly represents Jesus' mind on the matter as we find it in Q and Mark. Thus Dodd writes:

71

John's formula 'The hour cometh and now is', with the emphasis on the 'now is', without excluding the element of futurity, is, I believe, not merely an acute theological definition, but is essentially historical and represents the teaching of Jesus as veraciously as any formula could.[41]

Now for the question of christology. Is the Christ of St John basically different from the Christ of the synoptics?

Certainly Mark and John had no idea that they were commending different Christs. As Mark's title indicates, his gospel was about 'Jesus Christ the Son of God'. Similarly, John wrote to foster saving faith in Jesus Christ as the Son of God (John 20.31). Nevertheless, it has long been held that John gives us a divine being who makes claims for himself far transcending those made by the Synoptic Christ. Is this really so?

Discussing this question, John Robinson notes that 'in all four Gospels we have the paradox that Jesus makes no claims for himself in his own right, and at the same time makes the most tremendous claims about what God is doing through him'.[42]

Robinson has overstated a good case. Thus, when he says that Jesus never claimed to be the Son of God, he wrongly dismisses much excellent evidence in the gospels (e.g. Mark 13.32; Matt. 11.27 Q) that Jesus knew himself to be in a unique filial relation to God his Father. But we should agree that in the synoptic gospels the dominant stress falls on what God is doing through Jesus.

The apostles took the same line. Their message was never, 'This man went about saying he was the Son of God'; it was, 'This Jesus whom you crucified God has made Lord and Christ' (Acts 2.36).

John simply deepens this paradox. 'In John's Gospel,' says C. K. Barrett, 'Jesus is not a figure of independent greatness; he is the Word of God, or he is nothing at all.'[43] Again and again the Christ of St John says, 'If I claim anything for myself, do not believe me.'[44] On the other hand, he just as surely says, 'No one comes to the Father but by me.' He does not claim to be God – no, but he does claim to bring God, completely and finally.

What John does, then, is to bring out the full implications of the common tradition about Jesus. And yet he does more, for time and time again he gives to the whole picture dimension and depth. 'When all things began, the Word already was' (John 1.1 NEB), he begins his gospel, setting the whole story of Jesus in the context of eternity. Consequently, his theological contribution is not just another bit of the jig-saw puzzle – though, as we have seen, it is most certainly this; rather is it (as Robinson says) 'the piece which shows that the others (i.e. the synoptics) go to make up not merely a map but a globe'.[45]

'If John,' wrote T. W. Manson, 'had been confronted with the Synoptic Gospels and our estimate of them he might well have replied that 'fules and bairns shouldn't see half-done work' – that the Synoptics get their full significance only when their story is interpreted in the light of what followed, and that this interpretation is supplied by his own work.[46]

The purpose of this chapter has been to show that we may now use the Fourth Gospel with new confidence as a historical source. But we have also been suggesting that it depicts the person and work of Christ in depth, by giving us the true key to the rather episodic materials found in the synoptics.

For a long time John's Gospel has been, in the words of Sir Edwin Hoskyns, 'the text-book of the parish priest and the inspiration of the straight-forward layman'.[47] In the light of all we have said, we suggest that the New Testament scholar may now use it with new confidence, both as historical source and as interpretation.

12

The Gospel within the Gospels

Were a vote taken among Christians to decide the greatest verse in the Bible, there is little doubt that the sixteenth verse of the third chapter of John's Gospel would emerge an easy first. Why should these words strike a universal chord in Christian hearts?

It is because somehow their Christian instinct tells them that here, in one glorious verse, is the heart of the gospel, 'the gospel within the gospels', as Martin Luther pronounced it.

This is not to deny that the Bible contains elsewhere a wealth of human wisdom well fitted to guide our erring footsteps through this riddling and uncertain world. But weak and sinful men and women – and that such we are, the wrongness of the world and the sickness of our society today all too sadly and plainly show – when they turn to the Bible, want more than merely human wisdom. They want help from higher places. They want the assurance that in all their sins and sorrows the great being they call God really and veritably cares about their condition, nay more, that he has done something – something great and God-like – to lighten their darkness and to heal their hurts.

And it is just this message, this assurance, this word from the beyond for their human predicament that St John has written for them in words which age cannot wither or custom stale.

'God so loved the world' – 'the world', observe, our wayward, blundering, sin-sick humanity – and not a mere bouquet of select believers – so it begins.

I doubt if we Christians ever wonder enough at the tremendous truth on which our Faith is founded – the love of God. Sometimes we talk about it in all too sentimental ways, forgetting that the love of God is *holy* love, a love which cannot palter with our sin but must deal with it, as he did at Calvary.

Oftener we simply take God's love for granted as if it were something obvious and plain, like the sun in the sky. Yet God's love is not a truth of natural religion. It is not a conclusion that any thinking man might reach for himself, say, by studying Nature. On the contrary, if you and I believe in God's love, it is because at the cross we have seen, as through a window, into the heart of eternal God, and been moved to cry with James Denney 'God loves like that!'[48] or with Isaac Watts, in his hymn,

> Love so amazing, so divine
> Demands my soul, my life, my all.

'God is love' – that is indeed a precious truth, but it is not the gospel. 'God so loved the world that he gave' – that *is* the gospel. Only a love – be it human or divine – that authenticates itself in deeds, is worthy the name of love. A man may protest his love for you in a dozen fine phrases; but if that man never lifts a finger to help you in your hour of need, you will suspect – and rightly – his professed love for you. Love must prove itself in act and deed.

Now it is the very heart of the gospel that God so loved us, poor, sinful creatures of a day, that he did something, something infinitely costing to himself: God gave.

Gave what? Gave up his only well-beloved Son – gave him up to be born of woman, to take our nature upon him, to taste our griefs and temptations, and at last to die an accursed death, through and for our sins.

When we try to imagine what that gift must have cost God, we are driven, perforce, to fall back on human analogies. When St Paul thought of it, he thought of Abraham who 'spared not his own son' in the Genesis story (Gen. 22; Rom. 8.32). So today we think perhaps of fathers who have given only sons in time of national peril. Some of us recall Harry Lauder's story about New York in the Great War: the story of the little lad and his father walking the streets of the city when suddenly the lad espies a star cut in a window, and seeking an explanation, is told that the star means that that family has given a son in the war; and how later, as father and son come out, in the gloaming, into the open, the lad espies a single bright star in the evening sky, and with a child's flash of inspiration that goes deeper than he dreams, cries out, 'Look, Daddy! God must have given his own son too.'

'Out of the mouths of babes and sucklings', all unwittingly, the heart of the gospel!

Why did God give his only Son? 'That everyone who believes in him should not perish,' answers St John.

Dwell a moment on that word 'perish'. There is still today a bit of the old Pharisee in many of us which makes us think that we are too good for God to damn, or God too soft to condemn us. We reluct at the very idea that we could become lost souls. What then does it mean to perish?

Since true religion is fellowship with the unseen God, or, in the Bible's phrase, 'walking with Him', to perish means by our inveterate sinning, to forfeit that fellowship for ever. Exclusion from the presence of God, that, and not torment in everlasting flame (as many of our forefathers believed) is the fundamental idea in a Christian concept of hell. 'The everlasting absence of God and the everlasting impossibility of returning to his presence,' that, declared John Donne, is 'the hell of hells'.[49] Of the same mind, centuries later, was his successor in the Deanery of St Paul's, W. R. Inge.[50] 'The appropriate punishment for evil,' he wrote, 'is not to be cooked in an oven but to become incapable of seeing God, here or hereafter.'

This, and not writhing in eternal fire, is *the* truth about hell to which a Christian theology must hold fast, as Wolfhart Pannenberg has said.[51] We may not say that such exclusion from God's presence can never befall a man who, by his continual and unrepented sinning, alienates himself from the holy love of God. But, equally, it is not our business to say who, or how many, may suffer this fate.

76

So to the last words of 'the gospel within the gospels': 'that whoever believes in him should not perish but have eternal life.'

Observe that the adjective here in the original Greek is *aiōnios*, 'eternal'; not *aidios*, 'everlasting'. What is the difference? 'Everlasting life' is a matter of mere duration, means simply 'going on and on for ever' (like the brook in Tennyson's poem), which could be endlessly boring. By contrast, 'eternal life' deals in quality, not mere quantity. Life with the tang of eternity about it is what it suggests. It is a life lived in fellowship with God, through Christ who is its mediator, life which begins here and now but which, since it is God's own life, can never die.

If you ask me to describe it further, what can I do but point you to a great multitude who, through faith in Christ, have found, even in this present life with all its griefs and graves, a fellowship which transcends all earthly fellowships, a peace which the world cannot give or take away, and a call to care for others which moves them to 'brother all the souls on earth'.

'All this – and heaven too' is eternal life. Life that is life indeed, life continually spending itself in love, yet never diminished, life that 'age does not weary or the years condemn' – in a word, new, rich, radiant life here and now, and, after death, life beyond all hope of telling wonderful in a Father's 'house' with 'many rooms'. This is life eternal. This is the gift God offers in Christ his crucified and living Son to all who truly put their trust in him.

13

The Politics of Christ

'Politics,' declared Edmund Burke, 'should not be heard in the pulpit. There the only voice which should be heard is the healing voice of Christian charity.'

Christians who hold, like Burke, that politics and religion should be kept strictly apart, generally appeal to Christ's words about the tribute money: 'Give to Caesar the things that are Caesar's, and to God the things that are God's (Mark 12.17). They take them to be a judgment of Solomon neatly separating church and state – religion and politics – into two quite separate spheres.

This is to misinterpret what Christ said. When the Pharisees and others, trying to trap him, asked, 'Should we pay taxes to Caesar or not?', he replied, 'Fetch me a *denarius*' i.e. the silver coin with the Roman Emperor's head on it. 'Whose image is this?' he asked them. 'Caesar's,' they replied. 'Then,' said Jesus, 'give to Caesar what belongs to him.' He implies that they are his due, because (as Paul put it) 'the powers that be are ordained of God'.

But it is the second half of Christ's reply which carries the main weight: 'Give to God what belongs to him.' The real parallel to the *denarius* is man 'made in the image of God'. What he is saying to his inquisitors is this: 'The image printed on you – though you have apparently forgotten it – is not Caesar's but God's. You belong to him, and his claim on you is paramount. For Caesar's reign is transient, but God's sovereignty does not pass away.' It is another way of saying, 'Seek first the kingdom of God.'

Politics bulk larger in the gospels than most people suppose.

We cannot rightly understand many of our Lord's sayings without a knowledge of the political situation in Galilee and Judaea and, above all, of the growing clash between little Israel and mighty Rome which culminated in AD 70 with the destruction of Jerusalem.

Militant nationalism was no new phenomenon. From the time of the heroic Maccabees Israel had had its 'freedom fighters'. Then the enemy had been Antiochus Epiphanes who had turned the Jewish temple into a sanctuary of Zeus. In Jesus' day the enemy was Rome. When he was about a dozen years old, one 'Judas the Galilean', whose war-cry was 'No tribute to the Romans!', had led an ill-starred rising against them (Acts 5.37). Nor was this the only revolt. Moreover, as Josephus the Jewish historian tells us, it was for political reasons, i.e. fear of insurrection, that Jesus' forerunner, John the Baptist, had been put in prison at Machaerus.

These militants were the men we know as Zealots. Extreme Pharisees, fonder of the sword than of the phylactery, they are probably 'the men of violence' (*biastai*) in Matt. 11.12 whose aim was to establish God's sovereignty by force of arms. Galilee in particular contained many such, and even among Christ's chosen twelve was one named Simon whom St Luke explicitly calls a Zealot.

It was to men of this frame of mind that Jesus addressed his parable of the seed growing secretly (Mark 4.26–29). With an irreligious solicitude for God, they would do God's work for him – at the sword-point. 'Not so,' Jesus rebuked them in his parable, 'the kingdom is God's work, not man's. Stage by stage, and irresistibly, whether man will or no, the seed of the kingdom grows to harvest. God is like the patient husbandman in my story. Leave the issue in his hands.'

For a second example of how politics hold the key to a situation in Jesus' ministry consider the feeding of the five thousand (Mark 6.30–42; John 6.1–15). Here we find ourselves at the climax of the Galilean ministry. The scene is the north end of the lake, whither, after the disciples' mission, enthusiastic 'converts' have dogged Jesus' footsteps. As his eyes travel over the five thousand – and the Greek word *andres* means 'men', not women and children – his heart goes out to them because 'they were like sheep without a shepherd'. But note what that simile imports. To us, it suggests a congregation without a minister. In the Bible it regularly means an army without a commander. What in fact met Jesus' gaze was 'a Maccabaean host with no Judas Maccabaeus to lead them'.[52]

Then Jesus makes this host sit down on the green grass 'in rows, a hundred rows of fifty each' – words which mean not picnic parties but military formations. His next actions with the bread and fish recall what later he was to do in a Jerusalem upper room with bread and wine. In short, what the narrative suggests is a Galilean Lord's supper, an acting-out of his own story about the great supper (Luke 14.16–24), with its invitation, 'Come, for all things are now ready.'

Here St John adds a comment (John 6.14f.) which illuminates the whole picture. When, he says, the men saw the 'sign' which Jesus had done, they tried to take him by force and make him a king (Messiah) after their own dreaming. What was being planned was a 'revolt in the desert' against Rome with Jesus as its leader.

That we have correctly caught the political overtones of the event is shown by Jesus' later actions. First, he 'compels' the disciples (some of whom may have shared the popular hopes) to put a lake's breadth between them and the militants (John 6.16ff.; Mark 6.45). Then he persuades the excited throng to disperse, before himself retiring into the hills for prayer.

According to John 6.66ff., after this abortive rising many of Jesus' followers deserted him, so that he turned sadly to the twelve, 'Do you also want to go away?' Peter answered: 'Lord, to whom shall we go? You have the words of eternal life, and we believe that you are the Holy One of God', i.e. the Messiah. It is St John's version of Simon Peter's confession at Caesarea Philippi (Mark 8.29).

We are now at a decisive turning-point in Christ's ministry.

Having suppressed the desert revolt, Jesus now, to escape from the dangerous enthusiasm of his followers, retired out of Galilee with the Twelve into the solitude of Caesarea Philippi. Messiah he knew himself to be, but no Zealots' 'king to slay their foes and lift them high'. God had called him to be his servant Messiah; and if he were to fulfil his divine vocation, there was 'death in the cup' which his Father had given him to drink. So the march southwards on Jerusalem, the central heart and shrine of Jewry, began . . .

To save his people, if that were possible, from doom and disaster, was his aim; yet, with prophetic insight, he saw them set on a collision course with Rome, wherein, unless they turned back, God would use the Romans as the agents of his judgment. So in parable after parable he sought to warn them of impending catastrophe.

'You can read the weather signs,' he said, 'but why cannot you discern the (political) signs of the time?' (Luke 12.54–56). 'You are like a man on the way to court with his opponent over some quarrel. Make your peace with him now before you lose your case and are cast into prison' (Luke 12.57–59). Later still, as graver grew the crisis, he said: 'You are like travellers as the sun draws near its setting. Act now before the daylight goes and the darkness comes down' (John 11.9f.; 12.35f.) 'There is yet a last chance to repent before disaster overtakes you' (Luke 13.1–9).

Alas, old Israel would not hear, or heed. As Jesus came in sight of the city, he 'wept over it', predicting its destruction by Rome (in terms drawn from descriptions of the siege and capture of Jerusalem by the Babylonians in 586 BC): 'Would that even today you knew the things that make for peace! But now they are hid from your eyes. For the days will come upon you when your enemies will cast up a bank about you and surround you, and hem you in on every side, and dash you to the ground, you and your children within you, and they will not leave one stone upon another in you, because you did not know the time of your visitation' (Luke 19.41–44) or, as the New English Bible renders the last sentence, 'because you did not recognize God's moment when it came'.

Only if we remember the politics of the time and the mood of the Jewish people under Roman rule can we make sense of what Jesus did on the first Palm Sunday. The key to his action is to be found in Zech. 9.9f. Centuries before the prophet had predicted that one day there should come to Zion a king, riding upon an ass, to show that his authority rested not upon military force but on his call by God to inaugurate a reign of universal peace. So Jesus chose to enter Jerusalem riding not on a horse (the beast of war) but on an ass (the beast of peace). He would foil, by his acted parable, all attempt at a militantly messianic welcome by the people, make clear that he was no Zealot Messiah bent on rebellion against Rome. Alas, the response which his entry evoked carried ominous nationalist overtones: 'Blessed is the coming kingdom of our father David!' cried the excited crowds. By his symbolic action in the manner of the Old Testament prophets Jesus had challenged the Jerusalem populace to re-think their ideas and hopes for their nation. Sadly, their hopes seemed still set on a show-down between Israel and the hated Roman oppressor. What followed in the first Holy Week is familiar. Here we need mention only the trial of Jesus, first before the high priest and the Sanhedrin, and then before the Roman governor. At the Jewish hearing, the charge against Jesus was that of blasphemy, i.e. an offence against their religion. But when they came to present their case before Pilate, his Jewish accusers had changed all this. Now the charge was that of 'subverting the people and of forbidding the payment of tribute to Rome' (Luke 23.2), and it was clearly political. When, after hearing their evidence, Pilate was still unconvinced of Jesus' guilt, the last card his accusers played had politics written all over it: 'If you let this man go, you are no friend to Caesar' (John 19.12 NEB). So Pilate condemned Jesus to death.

As Jesus set foot on the road to Calvary (Luke 23.27–31), the women of Jerusalem broke into a death-wail for him. His response was to raise a death-wail over the doomed city. Prophetically foreseeing the horrors in store for it, he cried, 'Weep not so much for me as for yourselves and your children!' Again, he is thinking of the future clash with Rome. Incorrigible Israel has kindled Rome's anger; and if the flame is hot enough to destroy one whom Pilate has found innocent, what will be the fate of Israel's guilty men in the coming judgment of God? Or, in his own words, 'if these things are done when the wood is green, what will happen when it is dry?' (Luke 23.31). Wicked tenants of God's vineyard Israel's rulers have proved themselves to be. Henceforward the vineyard will be taken from them and given to others (Mark 12.9).

Enough has been said to show how largely politics figure in the gospels. The politics of Christ (as we have called them) are not 'the party politics' of a modern democracy. Rather are they world politics played out under God, the Lord of history, who is confronting men, for blessing or for judgment, in the person of Christ his Son. Ever in the background is the element of the transcendent and eternal.

It is precisely the lack of this element in much modern Christianity which was the burden of Dr Edward Norman's Reith Lectures for 1978.[53] All too readily today (he argued) do churchmen the world over interpret the Christ event in terms of contemporary secular values, many of them dubiously Christian, allowing the secularized world to set the agenda for the church. The faith (he said) is being disastrously over-politicized as churchmen, re-defining it in terms of secular, and sometimes of Marxist, categories, are allowing the divine dimension (so clear in Jesus' thinking) to go by default.

Much of the blame for this he lays at the door of the World Council of Churches. Themselves infected by modern secularism, they are distributing their own sickness to their healthy offspring in Black Africa and Latin American lands like Chile and Brazil. The same tendency he detects in the United States, and particularly in President Carter's obsession with human rights, as if this were the only article in Christian faith.

Inevitably, Dr Norman has provoked vigorous dissent from those whom he criticizes, for example, the liberation theologians of Latin America whose gospel has Marxist overtones. In places it seems to us that Dr Norman, holding a good hand, has overplayed it, as when he charges, 'the churches now see human rights as the essence of the Christian message'. Nevertheless, if our account of Christ's politics is sound, Dr Norman's well-documented protest against the secularization of Christianity is timely and salutary. God's ways are not men's ways, and we should beware of identifying God's purpose as revealed in Christ with the shifting values of our modern society. Moreover, the modern advocates of political activism should never forget how easily and quickly ideals promoted for good Christian reasons may be superseded by others of a purely secular, not to say pagan, sort.

Only Christ remains unchanging, 'the same yesterday, today and for ever'; and to identify him with the passing enthusiasms of men is to risk losing him in the shifting sands of human idealism, however well-intentioned. Christ called to a kingdom which was not of this world (John 18.36), yet one which men can enter, while still on earth, by being 're-created' or, as Christ told Nicodemus, by being 'born again'. Accordingly, Christians should ever hold fast the divine dimension of their good news, lest in their zeal for the transformation of this passing world, they rob men of their bridge to eternity.

14

The Memory, the Hope, the Presence

What are we Christians doing when we partake of the Lord's supper or, as we usually say, take communion?

Of all the answers given to this question few seem to me to come nearer the truth than that of Principal Cairns of Aberdeen to an Anglican friend: 'A retrospect and a prophecy, with renewal of the covenant face to face.'[54] In other words, the memory, the hope and the presence.

First, the rite is a remembering. 'This do,' said Christ, 'in remembrance of me', or, as it has been translated, 'for my recalling'. Here it is important to get this business of remembering straight, biblically straight.[55] When the men of the Bible talk about remembering, they do not mean, as we usually do, a mere idea in the mind – a pale, neutral, bloodless memory. Biblical remembering is ever realistic and dynamic. To remember in the Bible's way is to bring something back out of the past into the present – to make it real and contemporaneous – so that it becomes once again living, actual and potent, for good or ill (cf. I Kings 17.18, where the widow says to Elijah, 'You have come to bring my sin to remembrance, and cause the death of my son.').

So it was above all when the Jewish family kept the Passover feast out of which our Lord's supper was born. For the Hebrew, to remember the Passover was to re-live – to be caught up again by a kind of corporate memory in – the Exodus from Egypt, that act by which God had delivered old Israel from their bondage. 'In every generation,' it was said, 'each one of us should regard himself as though he himself had gone forth from Egypt' (cf. Ex. 13.8).

85

But now, says St Paul, speaking for Christians, 'our Passover has begun: the sacrifice is offered, Christ himself' (I Cor. 5.7 NEB). What you and I, then, are called to at our supper is a like dynamic remembering of that second and mightier exodus (Luke 9.31) by which, through cross and resurrection, God broke savingly into history and set up his new covenant – his 'new deal' – for sinful men. 'This cup,' said Jesus in the upper room, 'is the new covenant sealed by my blood' (I Cor. 11.25).

'Were you there,' asks the negro spiritual – 'were you there when they crucified my Lord?' If you and I remember aright, as we sit at communion, we are there. The cross steps out of its frame in past history, and we re-enact the story of our redemption. We are 'there' with the Twelve in the upper room 'on the night in which he was betrayed'. We are there with John and Mary at the foot of the cross to see the Saviour die. We are there at the empty tomb on the first Easter morning to hear again the stupendous news: 'He is not here; he is risen.'

But, if at communion we look back, we also look forward. Thus did Christ himself on that April evening long ago. 'I will no more drink of the fruit of the vine,' he said to his disciples, 'till I drink it new with you in the kingdom of God' (Mark 14.25).

It is Jesus' *au revoir* to his followers. Death for him is imminent. Never again will he drink wine at an earthly meal. But he will drink it again in a new sort – a new kind (*kainos* is the Greek word here) – in the kingdom of God. Here he is not thinking of any kingdom to come in this vale of time and tears; he is thinking of the eternal, the supernal, kingdom, which is heaven. He is saying, 'I will not drink wine any more till I drink it with you in God's nearer presence.'

So too all our Lord's suppers ought to have a heavenly forward-look, ought to lift our thoughts to Christ's coming in the glory of his Father, to the church triumphant, and all the unimaginable glory of heaven. As Horatius Bonar put it:

> Feast after feast thus comes and passes by,
> Yet passing, points to the glad feast above,

Giving sweet foretaste of the festal joy,
The Lamb's great bridal feast of bliss and love.

Men have called the Lord's supper the iron ration of the Christian soldier which fortifies him afresh to do battle with the world and all its evil. And so it is. But it is no less the 'arles', or earnest, of the perfect fellowship of heaven.

Looking back and looking forward, memory and hope – but there is a third element in this sacrament which binds memory and hope together, and which alone entitles us to call it as we do – communion. It is the presence – the real presence – of the living Lord.

The Christ, whom we confess is no mere figure in an old, old story, no 'dead fact stranded on the shores of the oblivious years'. He is one who, by the miracle of the first Easter day, has become a ubiquitous Lord – a Christ who still comes, unseen but not unknown, through the Holy Spirit, wherever two or three are gathered together in his name.

He it is who gives and blesses in the supper which he ordained. The broken bread and the outpoured wine on the holy table are his 'love-tokens to his body the church' – signs which really convey what they symbolize because, as long experience has shown, they deepen and enrich the saving relationship between the Redeemer and his redeemed. For in this sacrament, still keeping troth, Christ offers us afresh the fruit of his finished work. Thus he renews the new covenant once sealed by his blood upon the cross.

Yet the renewing of the covenant is not his only. As we are his faithful followers and confessors, we renew it also. In this *sacramentum* – this sacred oath of allegiance – as long ago as the Roman soldier to his emperor – we engage ourselves afresh to him who is the high captain of our salvation.

What do we promise? We promise to follow ever more worthily in our Christian discipleship. We promise to be better and truer members of his working body which is the church. We promise to fight ever more bravely under his banner to life's end.

15

The Spirit gives Life

What is it makes a person, an idea, even a landscape come alive
for us and become a presence to which we feel impelled to
respond? We do not make the all-important first move. In every
encounter of this kind there has somehow been an 'anonymous
third party' acting as a go-between, setting up a current of
communication, activating us from within. Who, or what, is it?

To this invisible go-between power or being Christians give a
personal name. They call him 'the Holy Spirit'. They say that
this was the Spirit which completely filled the man Jesus Christ.
They identify it with the Spirit which later came upon his followers. It is he, the go-between God, who still today can make
our religion real to us. For the Holy Spirit is 'the beyond in our
midst', God in action here and now, God making the truth of
the gospel come alive for us.

Such, in brief, is the view of Dr J. V. Taylor in his book *The
Go-between God*, perhaps the best book on the Holy Spirit written
in our time.[56]

To say that for many today the Holy Spirit is the most unreal
part of their religion is to state the obvious. How very different
it was in the glad springtime of our faith, as we may read in the
Acts of the Apostles or the letters of Paul! Come to the New
Testament with really fresh eyes, and you cannot mistake the
enormous importance which the first Christians attached to the
gift of the Holy Spirit as something quite new, 'a kind of "wire-
less" between heaven and earth that was not there before'.[57]
Because of this 'anonymous third person' in their midst it was
possible for every Christian church to be a sort of replica of the

Galilean circle, with the living Christ still among them, messages continually coming and going. As for Paul, you can no more understand his Christian teaching without the Holy Spirit than you can understand our modern civilization without the existence of electricity.

For the Christian church all this began to happen on the day of Pentecost, the first Whitsunday (see Acts 2). On that day, we read, Christ's followers 'were all together in one place'. Of course they knew that by raising Christ from the dead God had done something utterly new and marvellous, with implications for mankind at which they could only guess in wild surmise. But as yet, they did not thrill (in Paul's phrase) 'with joy and peace in believing', or feel an urge to carry their good news to the wider world. Yet, that morning, seven weeks after the first Easter day, something tremendous happened, something which almost defied description, something which afterwards they could only express in terms of 'a rushing mighty wind' and 'tongues as of fire'.

If there is one experience difficult to express in words, it is man's encounter with the living God, as Isaiah in the Temple, or the writer of Psalm 139, or Blaise Pascal, knew only too well. Try to recall, if you can, the most vivid experience you have ever had of the presence of God, then multiply it tenfold, and you may begin to understand what happened to Christ's followers on the first Whitsunday.

The Spirit of God (and the word Spirit, in both Hebrew and Greek, means wind or breath) came upon these men, and gave each of them new life. What Pentecost did was to fuse individuals into a fellowship which in the same moment was caught up into the life of the risen Lord. 'The Spirit gave life' to them, not only as individuals but now as members of a new community, with a new task confronting them not among their own compatriots only but in the wider world.

The new Israel, the church of Christ, had sprung into dynamic existence; and it was all the doing of that puissant Spirit of God which prophets like Joel and Ezekiel had promised centuries before . . .

Oh, had I lived in that great day,
How had its glory new
Filled earth and heaven, and caught away
My ravished spirit too!

So Matthew Arnold, in the nineteenth century.[58] How many, depressed by the religious apathy all around them today, have felt his nostalgia! Yet the Pentecostal gift has not been withdrawn. It is we who have stopped believing in the Spirit's presence and power, so that the *Geist* (which is German for 'spirit') has gone out of our Christianity in this 'humanistic' twentieth century. It is no new phenomenon. In the rationalistic eighteenth century the same situation obtained, and even the church's leaders were affected by it. Was it not Joseph Butler, the philosopher and Bishop of Bristol, who told John Wesley: 'You pretend to extraordinary gifts and manifestations of the Holy Ghost. That is a very horrid thing'? To this the best answer was John Wesley's own great ministry which, by the judgment of good historians, saved Britain from the red revolution which overtook France.

Then, suddenly and unpredictably – for the Spirit, like the wind, 'bloweth where it listeth' – men have returned to 'the Lord and Giver of Life' (as the Nicene Creed names him), and the church, recovering its lost radiance, has experienced seasons of refreshment and renewal. It is this very phenomenon which is happening in many parts of Christendom today.

The names for it vary, but perhaps 'Neo-Pentecostalism' best describes it. Starting some fifty years ago among American negroes, the movement has spread rapidly over the United States, spilled over into Europe and Britain, and is now engaging the serious interest of the Roman church itself. By common admission, it is the fastest growing movement in the Christian world today; and wherever it has gone, it has helped to revitalize moribund churches and to promote warmer Christian fellowship. There is now a large literature on the subject, and every year sees the publication of new books about the Pentecostals. What is the secret of their success? They have gone back to the apostolic source of spiritual power. They have rediscovered the Holy Spirit.

Long ago, in Corinth, St Paul had to deal with a Pentecostal Christianity, and the reader may find his wise comments on it in I Cor. 12–14. No Christian has ever had a firmer belief in the reality and power of the Holy Spirit than the apostle; but, by the same token, he was fully alive to the possible dangers in Corinthian Pentecostalism and its evaluation of the Spirit's many various gifts (or *charismata*). Thus, though himself an expert in *glossolalia* ('speaking with tongues' in ecstatic speech which required an interpreter, if it was to be understood), he declares himself strongly in favour of spiritual gifts which build up the whole church, and with his usual sanctified common sense lays it down that 'all things must be done decently and in order', for 'God is not a God of disorder but of peace'.

Similarly, today there are in Neo-Pentecostalism features which many of us find open to criticism: e.g. the Pentecostals' emphasis on speaking with tongues as the infallible mark of possession by God's Spirit, their Puritanical ethics, and their uncritical fundamentalism. Yet what no one can deny is their manifest new life in the Spirit; and when that great elder statesmen of the world church, John Mackay of Princeton, declares, 'If it is a choice between the uncouth life of the Pentecostals and the aesthetic death of the older churches, I for one choose uncouth life',[59] many of us find an answering echo in our hearts.

What we in these older Western churches must realize is that God's gift to his people at Pentecost is still available today. As F. C. Burkitt wrote:

> The centuries go gliding
> But still we have abiding
> With us that Spirit holy
> To make us brave and lowly.

Somewhere above the low valley along which humanity today is toiling with weary and bleeding feet the rivers of life, which have their source in the Spirit of God, are still springing in the sun; and, as we long for a Christian renaissance, it is time to hark back to them.

Once, long ago, as St John tells us, there came by night to Jesus in Jerusalem a teacher in Israel named Nicodemus, curious to know more about the religious revival then sweeping the land. 'What you need, Nicodemus,' Jesus told him in effect, 'is such a re-orientation of your whole life as can only be likened to new birth.' 'Impossible!' replied the literal-minded Nicodemus, 'How can a man be born again when he is old?' Then, as the two men talked together, the night wind rustled about their place of meeting. 'Listen to the wind, Nicodemus!' said Jesus, 'Whence it comes and whither it goes is a mystery. Yet how real a power it is! So is God's wind, the Spirit. It offers you what you need.'

Are not many of us today Nicodemuses? Is there not in Christ's parable about the night wind a word of God for us? Too long, infected by the humanistic thought of our time, we have been making do with a Christianity utterly devoid of spiritual dynamic and that enthusiasm which is ever a sign of the Holy Spirit's presence and power.

Doubtless our churches today need restructuring in order to meet the challenges of the day, as our traditional ways of worship need some refurbishing. But the prime *desideratum* is for that change of heart which only the Divine Spirit can create.

So, to all dispirited Christians we say 'Hope hard in the Holy Spirit. It is the Spirit who gives life.'

16

On Spiritual Sunbathing

More and more nowadays prayer is becoming a lost art, as people sit down to their unblessed meals and tumble nightly into prayerless beds. So man made in the image of God – and for fellowship with him – renounces his birthright and reverts to the level of the beasts:

> For what are men better than sheep or goats
> That nourish a blind life within the brain,
> If, knowing God, they lift not hands of prayer
> Both for themselves, and those who call them friend?

One reason why many have ceased praying is that 'the world is too much with us'. In our daily scramble for bread and material things, and in our pursuit of pleasure, we leave ourselves no time to hear the divine command, 'Be still, and know that I am God' (Ps. 46.10).

A second reason why people have given up praying is that they have too narrow a notion of what prayer really is. It is the practice of the presence of God. But mostly they think of it as a spiritual penny-in-the-slot machine which ought to produce a bar of chocolate every time they use it. Then, if they do not get what they want, they react like the small boy who said, 'I will pray to God all this week for an engine, and if he does not give it to me, I will worship idols.'

Such people assume that they know what is best for themselves. It does not occur to them that the all-wise Father in heaven may know better, and has a divine right to say No to them, as he once said No to his own well-beloved Son in the garden of Gethsemane (Mark 14.32–36).

Let us see if we can enlarge and improve our ideas about the practice of the presence of God.

To the religious man prayer is what original research is to the scientist – by it we make contact with reality, with the last reality in the universe, God. Prayer is in fact the very life-blood of religion – or, if you like, our life-line with the unseen world which lies ever over and above the curtain of our senses. And the sense of God will quickly fade from the heart of a man who gives up praying.

Yet, when clerics utter this spiritual truism, they are accused of speaking to their brief. Therefore let us call a quite *un*clerical witness.

Most of us have heard or seen (on TV) Lord Hailsham. Quintin Hogg (to give him the name he got at his baptism) has one of the finest minds in Britain today. At Oxford University he got a 'Double First'. As a lawyer he has few peers. As statesman he has played a notable part in politics and narrowly missed becoming Prime Minister. As a young man Quintin Hogg was an agnostic. He is now, and has been for many years, a devout Christian.

In his recent autobiography, *The Door Wherein I Went*,[60] some of his very best pages are on prayer. If, he says, Christians believe in God as a Person, as of course we do, we ought to try to communicate with him, that is, to pray. Such prayer will include asking God for things – strength for one's own daily living, help for other people, courage to face crises in our own life or the nation's, and so on.

But (he says) is asking God for things the be-all and end-all of praying? Surely it is something more than just crying up the chimney of the universe for presents from a celestial Santa Claus. And here Lord Hailsham makes his first important suggestion. Think, he bids us, of prayer as *spiritual sun-bathing*. Now there is a fresh and suggestive way of thinking about the practice of the presence of God. When we pray, out of the darkness we turn our faces upward to the God who is light, that is, pure goodness (I John 1.5). In prayer, if we may so put it, we open the pores of our spirit to the radiance of God's presence, and allow his gracious power to revive us, as the sunlight revives the flower. Thus prayer serves as a kind of spiritual sun-lamp, and, as George Meredith truly said, 'Who rises from his prayer a better man, his prayer is answered.'

When and how ought we to do our spiritual sun-bathing? Night and morning are the usual times, and on our knees the conventional posture. But, in fact, we can do it at any time of night or day, and anywhere – in a motor-car, or even in the dentist's chair!

If sometimes God's presence seems to be withheld from us, we can remember that, once on the cross, the Son of God himself had the like experience (Mark 15.24); and if our petition is refused, we may recall that even a great saint like Paul got a divine refusal when he prayed for the removal of his thorn in the flesh: 'Three times I begged the Lord to rid me of it, but his answer was: "My grace is all you need; power comes to its full strength in weakness" '(I Cor. 12.8f. NEB). So persevere in prayer, like that determined widow in Christ's parable (Luke 18.1–8); and if you have stopped doing it, why, begin again!

Lord Hailsham confesses that he finds it hard to concentrate for long when he says his prayers. But don't most of us? We are like Christopher Robin in A. A. Milne's poem.

> Little boy kneels at the foot of the bed:
> Droops on the little hands little gold head.
> Hush! Hush! Whisper who dares!
> Christopher Robin is saying his prayers.

But is he? Listen:

> 'God bless Mummy' – I know that's right –
> Wasn't it fun in the bath tonight?
> The cold's so cold, and the hot's so hot –
> Oh, 'God bless Daddy' – I quite forgot.

What then can we do about it? 'Little and often,' says Lord Hailsham, 'is the answer.' And has he not the best of all authorities for so saying? Did not Christ tell his disciples that men 'are not heard for their much speaking' (Matt. 6.7)? And are not his own prayers as recorded in the gospels mostly short?

What matters in prayer is quality, not quantity. 'God be merciful to me a sinner!' The tax-collector's prayer in Christ's parable (Luke 18.9–14) was only seven words long. Yet it was enough to put him right with God.

Moreover, in every Christian's life there come opportunities for tiny *Te Deums*, spontaneous little thanksgivings to God. You may witness a wonderful sunset or some splendid act of self-sacrifice. You may be the recipient of some unexpected kindness, or experience some happy deliverance in a time of trouble. News may reach you of a decisive set-back to some evil enterprise or of some heartening advance of God's kingdom in the world. Then is the time to offer up a short 'Thanks be to God!'

When Lord Hailsham counsels, 'Little and often', I am reminded of what our forefathers called ejaculatory prayer. 'Ejaculatory' comes from the Latin word for a dart, *jaculum*, that is, a small man-guided missile. As you can shoot a dart upwards, short but weighty, into the skies, so, at any time, you can shoot up a dart-like prayer to your heavenly Father. In such prayer many a man has found the power to resist the onset of temptation. Said one such who had known the strong craving for alcohol, 'Ejaculatory prayer has kept me out of the public-house for the last five years.'

Daily prayer, then, is as necessary to the Christian's spiritual health as is his daily constitutional for his body. Was it not Robert Burns who, though he disliked 'three-mile prayers and half-mile graces', declared:

> A correspondence fixed with Heaven
> Is sure a noble anchor?

So, if you want your Christian faith to become real to you, never neglect your spiritual sun-bathing. Every day open up your spirit to the light and radiance of God's presence –

> Speak to him, thou, for he hears,

And spirit with spirit may meet –

and let his Spirit renew yours, as his sunshine revives the droop-
ing flower, and his gentle rain the parched ground. If you find
concentration a problem, let your rule be 'little and often'. Above
all, keep on praying:

> More things are wrought by prayer than this world dreams
> of . . .
> For so the whole round earth is every way
> Bound by gold chains about the feet of God.

17

Preaching Then and Now

After hearing his minister preach, an acquaintance of ours declared himself shocked by what he had heard. 'Do you know what he was telling us?' he reported indignantly. 'That it wasn't he who was preaching but God himself? Well, all I can say is that God isn't a very good preacher.'

'Some sympathy was due this irreverent man-in-the-pew, for his preacher, though a noted theologian, had a penchant for darkening counsel with long and learned words. Yet, in saying what he did, however unsuccessfully, he had the backing of no less a person than St Paul. If you doubt it, ponder II Cor. 5.17–21:

> When anyone is united to Christ, there is a new world; the old order has gone, and a new order has already begun. From first to last this has been the work of God. He has reconciled us men to himself through Christ, and he has enlisted us in this service of reconciliation. What I mean is, that God was in Christ reconciling the world to himself, no longer holding men's misdeeds against them and that he has entrusted us with the message of reconciliation. We come therefore as Christ's ambassadors. It is as if God were appealing to you through us: in Christ's name we implore you, be reconciled to God! Christ was innocent of sin, and yet for our sake God made him one with the sinfulness of men, so that in him we might be made one with the goodness of God himself (NEB).

Observe that God's reconciling work in the cross of Christ and the message about it are not to be separated. This is shown by the parallel clauses joined by 'and' in verse 18. It is confirmed by the explanatory verse 19: 'God was in Christ reconciling the world to himself . . . and he has entrusted us with the message of reconciliation.' And the point is clinched in the first verse of the next chapter where it is expressly said that the apostles 'share in God's work'.

Clearly for Paul the act of preaching is itself part of God's saving activity. It gets its authority from the fact that Christ himself speaks in the word of his ambassador, or – what amounts to the same thing – God makes his appeal through Christ to men, using the apostle as his mouthpiece.

Is Paul, then, alone in holding this high view of preaching? On the contrary, it has been the view of great Christian preachers down the centuries. 'The proclamation of the Divine Word,' declared Johann Bullinger, 'is the Divine Word.' 'Preaching,' wrote P. T. Forsyth, 'is the gospel prolonging and declaring itself.'[61] And James S. Stewart is of the same mind: 'The procla- mation of the Word belongs itself to *Heilsgeschichte* (salvation history) and is an integral part of God's continuous saving activ- ity.'[62] In short, all agree that Christian preaching is the dynamic medium through which God the Holy Spirit today *contemporizes* his redemption and offers men the chance of responding to it by faith – that faith which is a taking of God at his living Word in Christ.

Now let us dwell a little on what may be called the 'philosophy' of preaching, as it concerns our Christian knowledge of God.

Here we owe a deep debt to the Jewish theologian Martin Buber and his book *I and Thou*.[63] There is all the difference in the world, said Buber, between a man's attitude to other *men* and his attitude to *things*. His attitude to other men is a relation between persons: to things, it is a connection with objects. In the personal relation one subject – 'I' – confronts another subject – 'Thou'; whereas in the connection with things like, say, a type- writer, the subject manipulates an object.

For us humans, then, authentic existence – real life – comes to pass when a personal 'I' meets a personal 'Thou' in direct encounter or dialogue. Now this concept of personal encounter holds the clue to our knowledge of God, for this 'I-Thou' relation applies equally in the realm of religious faith. Here it stands for that encounter with the living God of which the prophets and the psalmists provide countless illustrations and examples. (Think, for instance, of Isaiah 6 or Psalm 139.) Indeed, the whole Old Testament might be called a dialogue between 'the speaking I' of God and 'the hearing Thou' of Israel, his elect but often rebellious people.

When we turn to the New Testament, all is centred on one decisive encounter or event – the coming of God to men in the person of Christ and the revelation therein of his saving purpose for the world (John 3.16). 'The Word' (the saving purpose of God) 'became flesh', i.e. a human being, writes St John. 'God has spoken to us in a Son,' declares the writer to the Hebrews. What both are saying is that Christ is God's 'Thou' to us men in our human predicament.

Moreover, when we put our faith in God's Christ, we are sharing not merely in a past event, 'an old, old story', but in something which is happening now, and something which will happen when it pleases God to consummate his salvation in that other and better world of which John the Seer gives us inspired glimpses in the book of Revelation.

It is this divine event or encounter which ought to be the burden of our preaching, as the preacher's witness to it by his spoken word is part of God's saving activity today.

Alway's God's approach to men is through *persons* or through history, which is, after all, the sphere of persons in various kinds of relationship. A true preachment, then, is not an essay, or a lecture, or a piece of mere moralizing. Ever, in one way or another, it should have as its dominant theme God's personal coming in Christ as it impinges on our human situation today. 'Do you never preach from John 3.16?' said a man to John MacNeill, the famous Scottish evangelist. 'Na, na,' replied John, 'I have *that* in every sermon I preach.'

'Preaching the word', as we call it, should always mean the impact of one personality upon another, since no written word or indirect speech can ever have quite the same effect as the living voice of a great preacher, be it a Savonarola, a Richard

100

Baxter, an F. W. Robertson, a C. H. Spurgeon, or a Helmut Thielicke.

Through his speech the preacher, as God's mouthpiece in Christ, should focus on me the hearer as a person, challenge my will, and call for my decision. In a word, preaching should be a God's 'Thou' addressed to my 'I', directing itself in appeal and succour to me the hearer, and summoning me as a sinner to repentance and 'newness of life' through Christ his crucified and living Son.

For, eternal as the gospel is, there must ever be a *couching of it in contemporary terms*, if it is to come home to men's business and bosoms.

Moreover, the preacher should proclaim the gospel not only as God's call to the individual, but also in terms of all the problems and perplexities which vex our society today. What, then, are the chief malaises of man in this twentieth century?

Is not one of them just a bleak sense of *the meaningless of existence*? For multitudes today, life is just one long struggle to make ends meet, enlivened from time to time by the excitements of the racecourse, the football field, or the Bingo hall. They have no sense of a divine purpose running through their life, no understanding of it as 'the vale of soul-making' (John Keats), no thought of it as God's discipline for something better beyond the bourn of death.

It is here that the Christian gospel can minister to their need, if only we can present it to them in ways and words that they can understand. For is it not the heart of our good news that behind this mysterious universe there is not a blind and inscrutable fate but a holy heavenly Father who so loved the world that he gave his only Son for its saving and who still today, through his Holy Spirit, 'cooperates with them in all things for their good' (Rom. 8.28)? In all this, God's purpose is to create a great family of sons and daughters living for ever in fellowship with him, and trained for their eternal destiny by the discipline of free probation on this earth. In other words, our life on this planet is a kind of education that God our Father puts us through

101

that we may be fit persons to enjoy all those blessed things which he has in store for those who love him and seek on earth to do his will.

In the second place, millions of people today have a *deep longing for security* and some spiritual rock on which to stand. They are like the inhabitants of those lands where earthquakes make the ground reel and quiver beneath their very feet. The belief of their Victorian forefathers in irresistible progress to perfection, born of the doctrine of evolution, has been rudely shattered; and the aftermaths of two terrible world wars have left them with the feeling that everything is in the melting pot, with who knows what awful possibilities (e.g. nuclear holocaust) lying in the womb of the future.

What has Christianity to say to those who are haunted by this sense of insecurity? It does not pretend, with an airy optimism, that 'all's right' with our world, or declare that man is fundamentally good. Far from it!

> Tis the faith that launched point-blank her dart
> At the head of a lie – taught Original Sin,
> The corruption of Man's Heart.[64]

In other words, the faith takes man's 'curse' quite seriously, insists that, if way to a better there be, our sinful human nature must be changed by divine grace.

But, if Christianity has no place for utopianism, it has an optimism all its own. It is the optimism which you find in the New Testament, in the beatitudes, in Romans 8, in the First Epistle of Peter, and in the book of Revelation. It is in fact what that modern prophet Reinhold Niebuhr called in his book a 'beyond tragedy' optimism, an optimism which can look into the present abyss of evil unaffrighted because it knows that the world's destiny is in the hands not of the Devil but of God.

Why, all down the Christian centuries, have God's best servants been so sure of God's good and gracious purpose for the world when so much that happens in it seems to belie their belief? Because of one fact – or rather, one person:

On Christ the solid rock they stand,
All other ground is shifting sand.

It is he, the eternal Son of God, incarnate, crucified and risen,
who makes the difference. In the fact of Christ they have found
the master-clue to the great drama which God is working out in
the affairs of men and which he is shaping, amid all the hurly-
burly of history, to a blessed consummation.

Perhaps no modern Christian has put the whole issue better
than Principal David S. Cairns during the last war: 'When your
feet are on the rock (he meant 'the rock of ages') you can exult,
even in the whirlpool.' It was the same Mr Greatheart who, as
he lay on his death-bed, said to his son: 'I have feasted richly at
the banquet of life.' 'There is real life and love coming, Davie,
so let's be thankful. It is wonderful to think of passing straight
from human to Divine Love.'[65]

Finally, to guide his faltering footsteps through the world,
modern man needs some *moral ideal* to signpost him on his pilgrimage and challenge him to nobler living.

What is the good life? Down the centuries Greek philosophers
and Hebrew sages have perpended this question and come up
with various answers. Still today bewildered modern man asks,
How ought I to live? His need is for what the moralists call some
absolute in conduct; for, lacking it, he tends to drift through life like
a rudderless ship.

How, then, does Christianity meet his need? It offers him the
person and teaching of the Church's founder. It claims that
Christ himself, in his earthly life, was that moral ideal incarnate,
the very embodiment of the way in which God meant us men to
live. 'He hath a daily beauty in his life,' said Iago of Cassio in
the play, 'that makes me ugly.' Do we not feel the same when
we stand before the character of Christ as revealed in the gospels?
In that life of which they tell, do we not encounter goodness,
courage, magnanimity, gentleness and truth such as we find in
no other born of woman?

Nor is this all. In his own teaching – in the Sermon on the
Mount and elsewhere – he tells us how God means us men to

live. For Christ, *agapē* – a selfless and sacrificial 'caring' for others – is the master-key of morals. He teaches that true greatness lies in readiness to serve (John 13.1–17). And he sums all up in his Golden Rule: 'Always treat others as you would like them to treat you' (Matt. 7.12, NEB).

Yet this is but half the truth. Christ not only shows us what the good – the God-like – life is; he helps us with the living of it. For what is the Holy Spirit but Christ's own presence in spirit? And, as he promised to be with his people 'to the end of the world' (Matt. 28.20), does not this Christ, as T. W. Manson put it, 'still today have two hands',[66] one to point the God-ward way, the other to help his followers climb the steep ascent to heaven?

Thus, in three different ways, the gospel can minister to the problems and perplexities of modern man. It can put meaning – *eternal* meaning – into lives which otherwise were meaningless and empty. It can supply a 'rock of ages' on which to stand secure when the floods and storms of life are like to overwhelm us. Finally, amid the moral chaos of our times, it can provide not only a pattern for life but a divine Master to help us with its living.

Are not these the gospel themes which ought constantly to be on the lips of those who today are called to be ambassadors for Christ?

18

The Church's Song

Canticles, as we call them, like Mary's *Magnificat* and Simeon's *Nunc Dimittis* at the beginning of Luke's gospel, serve to remind us that Christianity began in song. And the Christian church which sprang from the church of the Old Testament – 'fairer daughter of a fair mother' – may be said to have gone on its great way singing 'hymns and spiritual songs'. Not that the first Christians stopped chanting the Psalms of David which had been old Israel's hymn-book: for was not Jesus Christ 'great David's greater Son', the fulfiller of Israel's age-long hope of a Messiah or Saviour? Yet, with Christ's coming and the dawning of his Father's kingdom, a new world of truth had swum into their ken, so that they felt moved to tell in 'new songs' how God had 'visited and redeemed his people'.

Some of these 'new songs' – or verses from them – you will find in the New Testament, like the Christ hymn in Phil. 2.6–11 which begins:

> Though in God's form he was,
> Christ Jesus would not clutch
> at parity with God,[67]

or that quoted in II Tim. 2.11, which was probably sung at baptism:

> If we with him have died,
> With him to live we rise,
> If we but firm endure,
> A throne with him our prize.

And the book of Revelation contains several noble doxologies like 'the song of Moses and the lamb' (Rev. 15.9ff.).

The second century had not long begun when, as Pliny the Roman writer records, hymns in praise of Christ were being sung at dawn near the shores of the Black Sea. And so, in succeeding centuries, as the gospel 'flew like hallowed fire from soul to soul', from Syria and Alexandria in the East to Milan and Rome in the West, the singing went on. Thus, from Spain in the fourth century and the Latin poet Prudentius came a sublime hymn on the incarnation (translated for us by J. M. Neale):

> Of the Father's love begotten
> Ere the worlds began to be.

From Ireland, in the fifth century, we have St Patrick's famous 'Breastplate', said to have been sung as he and his men went into battle against Leary the pagan king of Tara. To the same century belongs the majestic *Te Deum laudamus*, by many good judges accounted the greatest of all our hymns, and a perfect illustration of the dictum that our creeds were better sung than said. To St Gregory the Great, the Pope who sent Augustine to evangelize England, is ascribed the fine morning hymn, 'Father, we praise thee now the night is over' (tr. Percy Dearmer). And, meanwhile, 'breaking the silence of the seas among the farthest Hebrides', St Columba was chanting 'Christ is the world's redeemer'.

Even in the so-called 'dark ages' the song of Christian praise was not stilled. To the ninth century belongs 'Come, Holy Ghost, our souls inspire' (*Veni Creator Spiritus*). It was to have an enduring vogue, and modern Christians still sing it with fervour.

Passing to the twelfth century, we find Bernard of Cluny (in France) writing 'Jerusalem the golden, with milk and honey blest' (tr. J. M. Neale), while in Italy St Francis was inditing 'All creatures of our God and King' (tr. W. H. Draper). A century later, a follower of his, Thomas of Celano, penned the sombre *Dies Irae* with such verses as:

> Think, good Jesus, my salvation

Caused thy wondrous incarnation,
Leave me not to reprobation.

Faint and weary thou hast sought me,
On the Cross of suffering bought me,
Shall such grace be vainly brought me? (tr. R. Bridges).

Not much later, Bianco da Siena of Venice was invoking the Holy Spirit in a hymn which, in its English translation by R. F. Littledale, abides a favourite today, 'Come down, O love divine'.

Then, in the sixteenth century, came the Reformation, bringing with it a great effusion of Christian song. Here Luther led the way with his Christian Marseillaise *Ein' feste Burg*, vigorously translated by Thomas Carlyle, 'A safe stronghold our God is still'.

But Luther did more – much more – for hymnody. Helped by sympathizers with musical gifts, he laboured to produce *new* hymns which were then set to the tunes of those popular songs in which Germany has long been rich. Thus there broke forth in Reformation lands a mighty outburst of hymns proclaiming God's grace in Christ in the tongue of the common people. Small wonder that Luther's arch-enemy the Roman Cardinal Cajetan was driven to confess, 'By his songs Luther has conquered us.'

Hardly conducive to hymn-writing might seem the religious strife and civil wars of the seventeenth-century; yet through them Christians kept singing. Fine poets there were among them, notably the gentle George Herbert with his, 'Teach me, my God and king, in all things thee to see', and the Welsh physician Henry Vaughan with his, 'My soul, there is a country far beyond the stars'. The great Puritan Richard Baxter gave us 'Lord, it belongs not to my care, whether I live or die', and Samuel Crossman a moving lyric about Christ, 'My song is love unknown, my Saviour's love to me'. To Bishop Thomas Ken we owe 'All praise to Thee, my God, this night' and the morning hymn 'Awake, my soul, and with the sun'; and to the Baptist, John Bunyan, 'Who would true valour see, let him come hither'.

Not until the rationalistic eighteenth century did a springtime of song, like Luther's in Germany, come to Britain. Then none did more to set Christians singing their faith than Isaac Watts and Charles Wesley: the first a delicate little Congregational minister: the second, brother to John the great founder of Methodism.

Watts it was who opened the sluice-gates to let the stream of congregational praise go free. Composer of some six hundred hymns, he lives for most as the writer of 'O God, our help in ages past', 'Jesus shall reign where'er the sun', 'There is a land of pure delight', and that hymn which Matthew Arnold pronounced the finest in the English language, 'When I survey the wondrous cross'.

When the Wesleyan revival came to Britain, none saw more clearly than Charles Wesley that the best way to teach Christian truth was to set people singing it. From his pen, too, flowed six thousand hymns to serve the evangelism of his brother John as, for half a century, he rode up and down the land, preaching to common people and organizing his converts into Christian societies.

How much poorer our hymn-books today would be without 'Hark, the herald angels sing', 'O for a thousand tongues to sing', 'Jesus, lover of my soul', 'Christ the Lord is risen today', 'Let saints on earth in concert sing', and 'Love divine, all loves excelling'.

And what Isacc Watts and Charles Wesley did for England, William Williams, 'the sweet singer of Wales', did for his countrymen. To this day millions thrill to his 'Guide me, O thou great Jehovah', to the tune Cwm Rhondda.

Nor were these the only notable hymn-makers in this century. From the strict Calvinist Augustus Toplady came 'Rock of ages', that favourite with Gladstone and the Victorians. William Cowper wrote 'God moves in a myserious way' and 'O for a closer walk with God', while his friend and collaborator in the *Olney Hymns*, John Newton, is today chiefly remembered by 'How sweet the name of Jesus sounds', 'Glorious things of Thee are spoken', and, of course, 'Amazing Grace'.

Moving into the nineteenth century, we find ourselves in a time when a new spirit of intellectual enquiry was abroad and many old beliefs were being called in question. In face of these challenges to religious faith, some, declaring war on 'the spirit of the age', were fain to hark back to an idealized Catholicism of earlier days. Leader in this so-called 'Oxford Movement' was John Keble, who wrote the splendid morning hymn, 'New every morning is the love our wakening and uprising prove'. Keble did not leave the Church of England; but his great disciple, Newman, author of 'Lead, kindly Light' and 'Praise to the holiest in the height', took the road to Rome.

On the opposite Anglican front stood Charles Kingsley, a robust Protestant to whom we owe 'From Thee all skill and science flow'. Between them were men like Reginald Heber, composer of the Trinitarian hymn, 'Holy, holy, holy, Lord God almighty'; H. F. Lyte, author of 'Abide with me' and 'Praise my soul, the King of heaven'; H. H. Milman, whose hymn 'Ride on, ride on, in majesty' is still a Palm Sunday favourite; and John Ellerton, whose 'The day thou gavest, Lord, is ended', ranks among our finest evening hymns.

William Whiting is remembered by 'Eternal Father, strong to save', Edward Plumptre by 'Thy hand, O God, has guided', Sir John Bowring by 'In the Cross of Christ I glory', and S. Baring-Gould by his martial 'Onward, Christian soldiers', set to the music of Sir Arthur Sullivan.

Hymn-writing had now ceased to be only a male accomplishment. Here the Taylor sisters, Jane and Ann, were the pioneers with their hymns for children. After them came others like Frances Havergal with her 'Take my life and let it be', Catherine Winkworth with her 'Now thank we all our God' (translated from the German of Martin Rinkart), and Christina Rossetti with two exquisite Christmas carols, 'In the bleak mid-winter' and 'Love came down at Christmas'. Ironically enough, if Canon Greenwell lives today as the inventor of a celebrated trout-fly, his sister Dora is remembered by her hymn about the cross: 'I am not skilled to understand'.

If, during this time, Scotland's contribution to hymnography was less distinguished, one main reason was her people's continuing affection for the metrical psalms and the paraphrases. Probably her finest hymn-writer was Horatius Bonar, an Edinburgh man whose gospel songs include 'I heard the voice of Jesus say', 'Fill thou my life, O Lord my God, in every part with praise', and that favourite at communion: 'Here, O my Lord, I see thee face to face'.

Others there were like James Montgomery who gave us 'Hail to the Lord's anointed'; Walter C. Smith, author of 'Immortal, invisible, God only wise'; the blind poet-preacher George Matheson, writer of 'O Love that wilt not let me go'; and the two Macdonalds: George Macdonald whose 'O Lord of life, thy quickening voice awakes my morning song' makes a splendid hymn to begin the day with; and Mary Macdonald of Mull, whose Gaelic hymn, done into English by Lachlan Macbean, we know as 'Child in the manger, infant of Mary'.

Ireland has long been the motherland of poets and singers; and translated from the ancient Irish we have that modern favourite 'Be thou my vision, O Lord of my heart'. Among later Irish hymn-writers two names stand out. One is Thomas Kelly, a learned and humble divine whose liberality, during the Irish years of famine, won him the love of the Dublin poor. To him we owe two noble hymns, one about the cross, 'We sing the praise of him who died', the other about Christ's exaltation, 'The head that once was crowned with thorns is crowned with glory now'.

Yet beyond question the greatest name in Irish hymnology is a woman's. Cecil Frances Alexander was wife to the Primate of all Ireland. Her hymns, many expressly written for children, include 'All things bright and beautiful', 'Once in royal David's City', 'Jesus calls us! O'er the tumult', 'Spirit of God that moved of old', 'I bind unto myself today the strong name of the Trinity' (her version of St Patrick's 'Breastplate') and perhaps our finest hymn about the atonement: 'There is a green hill far away'.

Biblical and beautiful, clear in doctrine, her hymns combine the plainness of Isaac Watts, the Taylor sisters' feeling for and with children, and the felicities of the English Prayer Book, so that, in Stopford Brooke's words, 'they remain unequalled and unapproachable'.

Meanwhile in the United States, and as if to show what a truly 'catholic' thing a modern hymn-book is, Christians of many denominations were writing songs of praise. From Bishop Phillips Brooks came, 'O little town of Bethlehem', for Christmas time. Ray Palmer, a Congregationalist, gave us 'Jesus, these eyes have never seen'. To the Quaker John G. Whittier we owe 'Dear Lord and Father of mankind'. 'Lord of all being throned afar' was the work of Oliver Wendell Holmes, in daily life a Harvard professor of anatomy. Nor, in this brief account of American hymnology, must we forget Julia Ward Howe's 'Battle Hymn of the Republic', or 'the Gospel Songs', many of them written by a blind lady named Fanny Crosby, associated with the Moody and Sankey evangelistic tours in America and Britain during the last three decades of the century. Two of Fanny Crosby's hymns, 'If I come to Jesus' and 'To God be the glory! Great things he hath done', remain favourites to this day.

Before we leave the nineteenth century, one further event must be chronicled, the publication in 1899 of *The Yattendon Hymnal* by Robert Bridges, later to become Poet Laureate. Most of his hundred hymns were his own translations from Latin and German originals which, as himself a skilled musician, he married to the music of old masters like Thomas Tallis and Orlando Gibbons. One of them, 'All my hope on God is founded', based on a hymn by Neander, the first poet of the Reformed Church in Germany, is surely destined to immortality.

So, to the twentieth century, with all its scientific triumphs and its human tragedies. Yet through a century of 'wars and rumours of wars' Christians have kept singing, nor have there been lacking writers to swell the treasury of the church's song. Three years before it began, Rudyard Kipling had sounded a sombre warning in his 'Recessional', with its refrain, 'Lest we forget, lest we forget'. G. K. Chesterton was to repeat it in his 'O God of earth and altar':

The walls of gold entomb us,
The swords of scorn divide,
Take not thy thunder from us,
But take away our pride.

Yet, in spite of all the catastrophes that followed, Christians, fortified by their faith, have still kept singing, as witness the 'Songs for the Seventies'.

Among modern hymn-writers perhaps none did more to enrich Christian praise than the Anglican Percy Dearmer, now remembered chiefly for two hymns: 'Father who on man dost shower', and 'Jesus good above all other'. Many others have contributed single hymns of merit, like Louis Benson's 'O sing a song of Bethlehem' and Jack Winslow's 'Lord of creation, to thee be all praise'. Our Easter praise has been enriched by Birch Hoyle's 'Thine be the glory, risen conquering Son' (translated from the French) and G. R. Woodward's 'This joyful Eastertide'. For Whitsunday, we have now Edith Clarkson's 'For the gift of God the Spirit, with us, in us, e'er to be'. John Oxenham has sung the universal outreach of the gospel in his, 'In Christ there is no East or West'; and, as if to illustrate it, we have from Narayan Tilak, an Indian convert from Hinduism, his touching song of Christian discipleship, 'One who is all unfit to count as scholar in thy school' (tr. Nicol Macnicol).

But, if one may judge from the Presbyterian *Church Hymnary, Third Edition* (1973), it is in hymns for children that our hymn-writers (most of them women) have best served the cause of Christian education. Here we need only instance Edith Agnew's 'When Jesus saw the fishermen in boats upon the sea', Alda Milner Barry's, 'Good Joseph had a garden' (see John 20.1–18), and Carol Ikeler's, 'The church is wherever God's people are praising, singing their thanks for joy on this day'.

One feature of modern hymnology seems to me wholly admirable. It has been well said (by P. T. Forsyth) that 'we are not saved if we are saved into neglect of a social salvation'; and perhaps it is in their social emphasis that our modern hymns differ most strikingly from those of the nineteenth century. You have only to read the first lines of many hymns dear to the Victorians – 'Jesus, lover of my soul', 'Rock of ages cleft for me' 'I need thee every hour' – to be struck by their one-sided individualism.

Now, while Christian faith generally begins singly in what our forefathers called 'decision for Christ', the New Testament knows nothing of a solitary Christianity or one which turns a deaf ear to a brother man in his need. Accordingly, not a few modern hymns resound with a passionate concern for social justice and the righting of this world's crying wrongs. One thinks of Scott-Holland's 'Judge eternal, throned in splendour' with its prayer,

> With thy living fire of judgment
> Purge this land of bitter things,

or of H. E. Fosdick's 'God of grace and God of glory', with its supplication:

> Cure thy children's warring madness,
> Bend our pride to thy control,
> Shame our wanton selfish gladness,
> Rich in goods but poor in soul.

And there are many more.

What (we may finally ask) should be the aim of a good hymn?

A hymn is a religious poem designed for singing; and what Wordsworth said about his verses applies also to hymnology. 'Every great poet is a teacher', he wrote, and went on to define the purpose of his poetry thus:

> To console the afflicted, to add sunshine to the daylight by making the happy happier, to teach the young and gracious of every age to see, to think, to feel and therefore to become more actively and securely virtuous.

Similarly, a good hymn ought to *inculcate Christian faith and practice*, not only proclaiming the gospel but enabling Christians to think and feel their faith better and so inspire the nobler living. If the hymn should never be too obviously 'didactic', teach it should gospel truth, the way of life which ought to follow from it, or the 'living hope' which is ours in Christ.

For, as all our great hymn-writers have realized, 'a song may reach him whom a sermon flies'. Still it abides true; and hymns ancient or modern – the glorious *Te Deum* or Sydney Carter's 'Lord of the Dance' – may often teach Christian truth better than many a prosing homily.

Yet hymns ought to do even more than teach. All true religion begins in experiences when men become memorably aware that the obvious world around them is not the only reality, that there is a bigger unseen world over and around us, invading this one, so that we cry, like Jacob at Bethel, 'Surely the Lord is in this place and I knew it not'. In other words, the essence of religion lies not in mere knowledge, or good conduct, but in *awe* – in our human response to the mystery of the divine – of God – breaking into our world and our lives.

In Christian terms, this means our response to 'the Father of an infinite majesty' who has revealed his grace and glory in Jesus Christ his Son, and who, by his Holy Spirit, still confirms it in our hearts today.

Our hymns ought therefore to be also *aids to adoration* – should help to take us into God's presence and make the earthly sanctuary, however humble, a forecourt of heaven itself.

And this, by the testimony of Christian experience, the great hymns may do. They can set the spiritual adrenalin flowing. For some, the hymn that does this may be 'the Shepherd Psalm' given noble Christian expression in H. W. Baker's 'The king of love my shepherd is'; for others, more sacramentally-minded, William Bright's great communion hymn, 'And now, O Father, mindful of the love'; for others of a more mystical temper, John Wesley's version of Tersteegen's hymn, 'Thou hidden love of God'; and for others yet again, Isaac Watts's paraphrase of Rev. 7: 'How bright these glorious spirits shine!'

Ever the end-result should be the same: as we sing them in congregation with our brethren, we should be borne 'on wings of song' into the presence of our heavenly Father and of his Son our Saviour, and join, with all the company of heaven, in singing:

114

To him who sits upon the throne,
   The God whom we adore,
And to the lamb that once was slain
   Be glory evermore.

19

'These Three'

'Three,' we say, 'is a lucky number.' Whether this is Christian language is another question, not to be discussed here. What is certain is that down the centuries men have found the idea of three-foldness – of triplicity – strangely satisfying. 'Three,' wrote Pythagoras, the Greek philosopher, 'is the perfect number.' 'A threefold cord is not quickly broken', declared the Preacher in the Old Testament (Eccles. 4.12). And, as Dr C. L. Mitton has pointed out, if you turn to the gospels, you will be surprised to discover how often Christ himself, in his sayings and parables, followed 'the rule of three' and dealt in triads.[68]

In the epistles also we encounter triads. According to St John, the snares of the world (i.e. human society as it organizes itself apart from God) are 'the lust of the flesh, the lust of the eyes and the pride of life' (I John 2.16). Yet unquestionably best-known of all the New Testament triads is 'faith, hope and love', or, to set the words in their correct spiritual order (as in Col. 1.4f. and I Thess. 5.8), 'faith, love and hope', since, as Bishop Light-foot observed, 'faith rests on the past, love works in the present, and hope looks to the future'. Since this triad is found in what is St Paul's best-known chapter, I Cor. 13, most of us naturally assume that this group of three was of Paul's inventing, as uniquely his as *Veni, vidi, vici*, 'I came, I saw, I conquered', was Julius Caesar's. Yet we are wrong in so supposing. Paul indeed uses the triad seven times, but it was current Christian coin before he wrote any of his letters.

Note, first, how Paul introduces it in I Cor. 13: 'faith, hope, love, *these three*', as if to say, 'You know, the well-known three'. Observe, next, the tell-tale way in which he uses the triad in what most scholars believe was his earliest letter, I Thessalonians, written about AD 50: 'Putting on the breastplate of faith and love, and for a helmet the hope of salvation' (I Thess. 5.8). Paul's figure here of the spiritual warrior he took from Isa. 59.17: 'He put on righteousness as a breastplate, and a helmet of salvation upon his head.' To be perfect for Paul's purpose, his source would have mentioned three pieces of armour – say, the breastplate of faith, the buckler of love, and the helmet of hope. Not finding the second bit of armour in Isaiah's metaphor, yet wishing to work in the three members of the triad, Paul had to write 'the breastplate of faith and love', and keep his second piece of armour for 'hope'.

Finally, the triad is not peculiar to Paul. We find it also in I Peter 1.3–8 and Hebrews 10.22–24, as well as in the Apostolic Fathers, where we have no reason to suspect dependence on Paul. We conclude that 'faith, love, hope' was a *pre-Pauline* Christian triad, which may even possibly go back to an uncanonical saying of Jesus, for St Macarius of Egypt reports as 'a word of the Lord': 'Take care of faith and hope through which is begotten the love of God and of man which gives eternal life.'

What is the importance of this? If (as Dean Inge once said) we can, by study, discover what words like faith, hope, and love meant to the first Christians, we shall be at the heart of the Christian revelation.

Before we attempt to do this, we must clear up another misconception. This one involves the traditional distinction between 'natural' and 'revealed' theology. Too long it has become customary to regard 'faith, love, and hope' as supernatural 'graces' which must be clearly distinguished from 'natural' virtues like justice, courage, and temperance. The first sort, it has been held, depend on the grace of God; the second are achievable by man's own effort. But can this radical distinction really be maintained?

Consider, to begin with, that other little word 'joy' which, according to the New Testament, is also one of the 'fruits of the Spirit' (Gal. 5.22). It was a fine saying of John Buchan's that 'the joy of being alive is an earnest of immortality'. By this he meant that the Christian hope of everlasting life has its root and promise in 'natural' *joie de vivre*, so lyrically described by Browning:

> How good is man's life, the mere living!
>   How fit to employ
> All the heart and the soul and the senses,
>   for ever in joy![69]

But is not this also true of 'fruits of the Spirit' like faith, love and hope? Are they not in fact mediated to us through ordinary human experience in which *faith interprets, love unites, and hope inspires*?

All men have faith in the sense that they cannot live without some object on which to fix their devotion, be it but a good football team or a fine racehorse. And is not faith, even at this very mundane level, a kind of intuition or 'knowing' which enables its possessors to understand better the objects of their devotion and forecast what they are likely to do.

So with love. If, in our daily living, hatred separates, is it not love which draws together? Man is so made that he cannot live alone, or, as the Bible puts it, 'it is not good for him to be alone'. And is it not a kind of love which impels him to seek union and fellowship with other mortals?

Yet love has no tomorrow, if hope there is none. For it is hope which ever inspires and beckons man on. If love reaches out for what it can see, hope, by reaching out for what it cannot see, helps to bring things to pass.

In human life, then, the so-called theological virtues of faith, love and hope are all necessary, each depending on the other. Since they have natural roots, we should not therefore sharply distinguish them from the common or cardinal virtues. The three graces central to Christianity as a revealed religion (which we propose to study one by one) have firm rootage in what we usually call natural theology.[70]

20

Christian Faith

Christians are – or should be – people who live by faith, work through love, and abide in hope. First, then, what do we mean by faith?

George Macdonald, the Scottish novelist and poet, to whom C. S. Lewis owed so much, somewhere pictures an old man in an ill-lit cottage calling a child in from the road. And she goes, groping and following the sound of his voice till she feels his hand on her head. 'Noo, my lass,' he says, 'ye'll ken what faith means. When God tells ye to gang in the mirk, gang.'

Are we not reminded of Abraham whom the Bible calls 'the father of the faithful'? When God told him to get up and leave his homeland, Abraham took God at his word and went out not knowing whither he went. And, as he lived out his long life, still believing, his faith made and kept him right with God.

Christian faith is like this – trust plus obedience – but with one decisive difference. For the Christian the mirk has been wonderfully illumined by the coming of Christ. But let us begin at the beginning.

Christianity is often called 'the faith'. But faith is no monopoly of Christians. It goes back to earth's origins, and would seem to have been engrained in all living things. When, as the evolutionists tell us, life first emerged from the sea, faith was already there. For what was there in all that the wisest little fish could know to warrant his belief that life would be better on dry land than in the water, or that his attempt to live on earth would result in his swim-bladder being turned into lungs for breathing?

Yet so it proved to be. Was that first little fish's venture of faith so very different in principle from Abraham's?

Or take another point. Today the humanists like to contrast religious faith unfavourably with modern science, as though faith were, as the schoolboy said, 'believing what you know ain't true', and science the only pathway to reality. What they forget is that, by the testimony of the scientists themselves (e.g. Lord Kelvin) every great scientific discovery has begun with an act of faith, with a postulate which no man could prove.

Moreover, nowadays we have even a science of religion, and very significant have been its conclusions. The first is that religion is a universal phenomenon; the second, that, however much the religions of the world differ, they contain three constant elements: one, the concept of the unseen ruling power; two, the belief that men can enter into communion with this power; and, three, the conviction that such communion leads to fuller life.[71]

Now let us see how this faculty called 'faith' can help to interpret the riddle of the world and the mystery of human life, to which Christians claim to have the solution in Jesus Christ.

To understand this claim, we must begin further back, namely, in the Old Testament, 'the cradle in which Christ was laid'.

In the millennium before the Christian era the Hebrews had come to certain conclusions about the unseen ruling power of which all religions speak. Chief among them was the conviction that the world had been created and was ruled by one God who was holy, righteous and good, and that he had entered with them into a special relationship, or covenant, because he had a high purpose for them to fulfil, namely, 'to be a light to lighten the Gentiles'. Israel was meant to be the school of knowledge of God to all mankind. If we ask how the Hebrews came to this great conviction, there can be but one answer: God had revealed it to them.

Such was Israel's faith as expressed by her great prophets, or spokesmen for God. By the light of it men like Isaiah and Jeremiah were able to make sense of the many disasters which befell the Hebrews in their chequered history. And out of this faith there sprang the expectation that in some blessed future time

120

God would send a Messiah, or Saviour, who would preferably reveal God's nature to them and deliver his people from their sins and woes.

The New Testament tells how this great expectation was fulfilled in the coming of Christ, the advent of the Holy Spirit, and the rise of the new Israel, the Christian church.

This is what we call the gospel, or good news of God, and the means of appropriating it, of making it our own, we call faith. What is Christian faith? As for Abraham it meant taking God at his word, so for Christians it means taking God at his living Word in Christ.

In the New Testament, what we call revelation is, to use the language of the cinema, not a still but a movie, an enacted drama. In this drama we do not get merely a picture of God: we get God himself in saving action. For 'God was in Christ reconciling the world to himself'. In Christ he himself came. The drama of which the New Testament tells has four acts:

1. The ministry of Jesus culminating in the cross.
2. The miracle of the first Easter day.
3. The coming of the Holy Spirit at Pentecost.

And act 4? The Christian drama is an unfinished one: the final act is yet to be played out at the end of history when God will consummate his great saving purpose in the glory of another and better world, of which John, the Seer of Patmos, gives us inspired visions in the book we call Revelation.

Now let us examine the nature of Christian faith more fully.

To begin with, it is directed not to a proposition but to a person – to Jesus Christ as the Son of God, and his perfect revealer. Faith means utter trust in the living Christ who died for our sins and who, though now reigning with his Father in heaven, still comes, 'unseen but not unknown', through the Holy Spirit; for 'the presence of the Spirit is Christ's own presence in spirit'.

This faith St Paul, our 'fifth evangelist', once summed up in one of his greatest sentences: 'The life that I now live in the flesh,' he wrote, 'I live by faith' (Gal. 2.20). What kind of faith? 'Faith in the Son of God who loved me and gave himself for me.'

How does a man come to a faith like this? 'Faith comes from hearing' (Rom. 10.17), hearing the gospel. And a man gets such a faith (for it is really God's gift) when he responds with his whole heart to God's good news in Christ for sinners. When a sinful man hears the story of the cross aright: when, as he gazes upon that strange man hanging there, he sees not just one more Jew dying a malefactor's death on a Roman gibbet, but the very God himself bearing in the person of his Son the sins of the world; when, as there breaks on him the revelation (it is the work of the Spirit) 'God loved, and loves, like that', what is that man to do?

If a man with the sense of his own sin and guilt upon him once sees the cross like that, there is only one right thing to do – to surrender himself to that sin-bearing love which confronts him in the cross, and to do so unconditionally, unreservedly, and for ever.

Yes, for ever. For Christian faith is not the act of a moment only; it is the attitude of a whole life. It is not merely once to stand up in church and say, 'I believe in God through Jesus Christ his only Son our Lord and Saviour.' It is to go on believing this day after day, year after year, and counting that the highest wisdom God has given you under his visiting moon. Christian faith is the grand venture in which we commit ourselves and our whole future to the conviction that Christ is the reality of God.

To make this grand venture is not to have all life's mysteries unveiled. Here on earth, like Paul, we see 'through a mirror dimly' (I Cor. 13.12 RSV). Not till, please God, we stand in the full light of eternity and 'see face to face', will the tangles of human life unroll and fall into shape. But to those who make the grand venture, the mysteries of this world are no longer mysteries of darkness; they have become mysteries of light; and by that light they can travel, lovingly and hopefully, till travelling days are done.

21

Christian Love

Christian faith, we have seen, means taking God at his living Word in Christ. If such faith is the deep root of the Christian life, love is its fine flowering. 'Faith works through love,' Paul tells us (Gal. 5.6) – finds expression in love, energizes in love – or it is nothing worth (I Cor. 13.2). What, then, did Jesus teach about it? How did he himself embody it? And if love is indeed the master-key of Christian morals, how can we Christians today live by the law of love in the so different world of the twentieth century? These are the questions we shall try to answer.

First, some linguistics. Whereas English has but one word, the Greeks had at least three for love. *Erōs*, or desire, was their word for love between the sexes. Next came *philia*, friendship, that is, mutual affection between kindred spirits. But the noun *philia* occurs but once in the New Testament; and, though, the Greek philosopher Plato had used *erōs* for 'the upward yearning for the divine and eternal', it is never found in the New Testament. The New Testament word for love is *agapē* and, either as noun or as verb, it occurs some 250 times.

What is *agapē*? It is the love which seeks not to possess but to give. If *erōs* is all 'take', and *philia* is 'give and take', *agapē*, is all 'give'. Unlike our word love, which nowadays can mean almost everything from Hollywood to heaven, *agapē* is neither erotic nor sentimental. The Authorized Version translates it in I Cor. 13 by charity, from the Latin *caritas* (which should mean 'the art of being a dear'). But charity will no longer serve as a good translation. Sadly, it has come down in the world of words. Today men say, with an accent of scorn, 'We don't want your charity.'

If there is a one-word equivalent in English for *agapē*, it is caring, caring for others because God has cared for us. The dying Baron Von Hügel surely thought so when he said to his niece Gwendoline Greene, 'Christianity taught us to care. Caring is the greatest thing. Caring matters most.'

Before Christ came, *agapē*'s history had been undistinguished. Classical writers never used it, and for later ones who did, it meant no more than 'having regard' for somebody. Then came the gospel, and at once this nondescript word was baptized with new meaning, as the Christians poured into it all the new grace and truth that had come to them with Christ.

A Greek philosopher like Aristotle thought it absurd to credit 'the great prime mover' (his name for God) with love. The Christians knew better. They had seen love incarnate and in action in a Man. 'God,' they said, 'is *agapē*' (I John 4.7) and he loved the world so much that he gave his only Son for its saving (John 3.16). More (they said), our Christian love for others is God's love reflected and responded to.

Now let us see how Christ and, after him, his apostles construe the word *agapē*.

The burden of the good news which Christ came proclaiming, and indeed embodying in his own person, was that God's kingdom, or saving rule, was now dawning and men must consider how to get into it. In this kingdom the King was a holy heavenly Father who willed that his children should live in a new way – the way of the kingdom. What was to be its basic principle, or *Leit-motiv*? It was *agapē*, that self-giving for others which we have called caring.

It has been truly said that Christ gave only one command – a twin imperative: 'Love God, and love your neighbour.' To do this was, for Christ, to 'fulfil the Law' (Mark 12.29f.). (When, later, Paul wrote [Rom. 12.10]: 'Love is the fulfilling of the Law', he was but echoing his Lord.) For most of Christ's other imperatives recorded in the gospels are but applications of the single law of love to the varying situations of life, e.g., 'Do not set yourself against the man who wrongs you', 'If anyone forces you to go one mile, go with him two', 'Give to him who asks', and so on.

Study Christ's moral teaching in the Sermon on the Mount (Matt. 5–7) or in his parables, and you cannot but remark how practically, unsentimentally and all-embracingly he construes the verb 'to love'. By loving he means caring actively and selflessly not only for the decent and the deserving but for all who stand in need of our help. Recall, for instance, how he once dealt with a quibbling lawyer (expert in the Law of Moses). 'How can I love my neighbour when I don't know who he is?' the lawyer had said to him. 'Real love,' replied Christ in his tale about the Good Samaritan, 'never asks questions like this. All it asks for is opportunities of going into action.' (In other words, it is wrong to construe Lev. 19.15 – 'You shall love your neighbour as yourself – in terms of 'neighbour'; you must construe it in terms of 'love'.)

But the crown of Christ's teaching about *agapē* is to be found in Matt. 5.43–48. There he carries all his teaching about it to its spiritually logical conclusion, love of people who, because they have wronged us, we count as enemies: 'What I tell you is this: Love your enemies, and pray for your persecutors. Only so can you be children of your heavenly Father who makes his sun rise on good and bad alike and sends the rain on the honest and the dishonest . . . There must be no limits to your goodness as your heavenly Father's goodness knows no bounds' (NEB).

Yet this is but half of love's story in the gospels. By the end which crowned his earthly work – by his self-sacrifice for sinners in obedience to his Father's will – Christ gave the word love a still richer meaning. For there in Jerusalem, first round a supper-table, then in a garden, and finally on a Roman cross, the supreme act of *agapē* had been accomplished.

Looking back upon that act Paul was to write: 'While we were yet helpless at the right time Christ died for the ungodly. Why, one will hardly for a righteous man – though perhaps for a good man one will even dare to die. But God shows his love for us in that while we were yet sinners Christ died for us.' (Rom. 5.6ff.).

Of the same mind was St John. 'Herein,' he wrote, 'is love, not that we loved God but that he loved us and sent his Son to be the expiation for our sins.' (I John 4.10).

Accordingly, as A. C. Craig has put the matter, 'the word "love" always needs a dictionary, and for us Christians the dictionary is Jesus Christ. He took this chameleon of a word and gave it a fast colour, so that ever since it has been lustred by his teaching and life, and dyed in the crimson of Calvary, and shot through with the light of Easter morning.'[72]

Here it is worth making a point too often forgotten. When St John declares that 'God is love' (I John 4.8,16), he does not mean that loving is but one of God's several activities. He means that *all* God's activity is loving activity. If he creates, he creates in love. If he rules, he rules in love. If he judges, he judges in love. In short, all that God does is the expression of his nature which is love.

Now, since our Christian love is really God's love reflected and responded to, it follows that St Augustine's summary of the Christian ethic, 'Love, and what you will, do' really means: 'If you hold your peace, through love hold your peace. If you cry out, through love cry out. If you correct, through love correct. If you spare, through love spare.'[73] In a word, all Christian activity, whether protesting, rebuking, sparing, or even on occasion just keeping our mouths shut, is, or ought to be, loving activity.

Now to sum up and apply all we have been saying about *agapē*.

First, 'we love because he first loved us'. Our Christian love is our response to the divine love shown us in Jesus Christ. 'Love came down at Christmas', sang Christina Rossetti. Therefore:

> Love shall be our token,
>   Love be yours and love be mine,
> Love to God and all men,
>   Love for plea and gift and sign.

Next, such love fulfils the Ten Commandments. But how, and why? Because the man who really cares for his neighbour will never dream of murdering him, or taking his wife, or stealing his property, or giving false evidence against him, or coveting his possessions.

Finally, such love ought to be the law of the Christian's everyday living, not just a theological virtue to be discussed, but something to be done. We are to 'put our love not into words but into deeds, and make it real' (I John 3.18, Moffatt's translation).

'Love never fails,' wrote St Paul in 1 Cor. 13. By this he doubtless meant that only love lasts on because love is the life of heaven itself. Yet we may fairly take his words also to mean that, however hard the problem, 'love will always find a way'. Often it will take courage and firmness, and on occasion it may even mean being cruel in order to be kind, like the doctor who says to his patient, 'This is going to hurt, but it is for your good.' But, whatever the circumstances, such Christian action will always have about it the quality of caring which is the very essence of *agapē*.

Such love Henry Drummond called 'the greatest thing in the world' because it has a capacity to sweeten human relations and to make the rough places plain which nothing else possesses. Who can tell how many religious rancours would be removed, how many racial tensions relaxed if men and women calling themselves Christians brought a little more *agapē* to the conference table or to their daily dealings with their neighbours. At any rate, our calling as committed Christians is plain. As by faith we take God at his living Word in Christ, day by day, in home, in office, on the shop floor, or in the community around our own doors, we are called to 'work through love'.

Not *erōs* but *agapē* it is which makes the moral world go round.

22

Christian Hope

If faith helps men to interpret the riddle of the world, and love unites them one to the other, is it not hope which inspires them to go on living? Might we not in fact call it the lifebuoy which the Almighty throws out to keep us floating on life's troubled sea?

To the reality of this hope, and our need of it, poets, philosophers and physicians alike bear witness. 'Hope springs eternal in the human breast,' sang Alexander Pope. 'What oxygen is for the lungs, such is hope for the meaning of human life,' wrote Emil Brunner. Says a noted American cardiologist, 'Hope is the medicine I use more than any other.' And is not this 'natural' hope the root out of which grows our Christian one?

To understand it, we must begin in the Old Testament. Rightly has the story of Israel been named a long 'Odyssey of hope', a hope which, century after century, survived one national disaster after another. Moreover, in the writings of their great prophets like Isaiah and Jeremiah it becomes a hope *par excellence*, the hope of a blessed future when God will make a 'new covenant' with his people, bring in his kingdom, and send his Messiah to be the bearer of his salvation to men.

In the providence of God the stream of that great hope was to run underground for more than five centuries. It was fulfilled at last in the reign of the Roman emperor Tiberius when Jesus came into Galilee proclaiming, 'The time has come, the kingdom of God is upon you; repent and believe the gospel' (Mark 1.15 NEB).

Followed the ministry in which Jesus, calling himself the Son of man, challenged old Israel to 'turn back' and accept his good news; and, at last, when words no longer availed, went, by the will of his heavenly Father, to the cross, in order to 'ransom the many' (which is Hebrew for 'all') from their sins (Mark 10.45). . .

When darkness fell on the first Good Friday, to all his followers it must have seemed the day on which the great lamp of hope which he had lighted was finally and for ever extinguished. 'We had been hoping that he was the one to redeem Israel,' said two sad travellers on the road to Emmaus (Luke 24.21), and they spoke for many more.

How wrong they were, the shining miracle of the first Easter day was to show. By God's mighty act Christ had left one gaping tomb in the wide graveyard of the world, and his triumph over the last enemy was an event whose consequences were incalculable. For if one, and he that one who carried in his own person the destiny of God's people, had exploded the myth of death's invincibility, there was life – new life and hope – in prospect for all who were his.

So hope was wonderfully reborn by Christ's resurrection. 'The world was growing old', wrote Mommsen in his *History of Rome*, 'and not even Caesar could make it young again.' But what Caesar could not do, the risen Christ did. In the Acts of the Apostles you may read how in three decades the heralds of the risen Lord carried the good news from Jerusalem to Rome. Impelled by the Pentecostal gift of the Holy Spirit, they proclaimed to all salvation from sin through the cross, membership in God's new people, the church, and, beyond death, the blessed hope of everlasting life.

Consider how Christ's apostles, or special messengers, describe the hope of the gospel. Paul speaks of 'the God of hope'. 'May he fill you with all joy and peace in believing,' he writes to the Christians in Rome (Rom. 15.13). Our Lord he names 'Christ Jesus our hope' (I Tim. 1.1). Christians, he declares, 'exult in hope of the glory of God' (Rom. 5.2).

St Peter opens his First Epistle to the Christians in Asia Minor with a paean of praise for Christ's triumph over death: 'Blessed be the God and Father of our Lord Jesus Christ! By his great mercy we have been born anew to a living hope by the resurrection of Jesus Christ from the dead, and to an inheritance which is imperishable, undefiled and unfading, kept in heaven for you' (I Peter 1.3ff.).

Hope, says St John, is a sanctifying virtue, 'for every one who has this hope purifies himself as Christ himself is pure' (I John 3.3). And the writer to the Hebrews, in a splendid metaphor, calls Christian hope 'a sure and steadfast anchor of the soul', because the risen and ascended Christ has himself made it fast for us in his Father's heaven (Heb. 6.19).

So they write, and in this ebullition of Christian hope one thing is plain. Never is New Testament hope a vague, woolly optimism, like Mr Micawber's, that somehow, in spite of all misfortunes, something will eventually turn up. Ever it is religious hope, hope which rests not upon mortal man but upon the living God who 'has broken the power of death and brought life and immortality to light through the gospel' (II Tim. 1.10).

Turn now to the world of today.

'What shape is the world, Daddy?', one enquiring young man is reported to have asked his parent. 'The hell of a shape', came the grim reply. We all know the world that father had in mind. It is the world headlined in our daily newspapers and every night reflected on our TV screens, the world which abounds with human devilry, and over which, like the Almighty's awful warning to humanity, impends the dark shadow of the hydrogen bomb. No wonder many despair of its future. Where shall we turn for deliverance from the depression which now lies, like a black frost, over much of humanity?

Shall we set our hope on communism? Will Marxism's secular hope supply what we so desperately need? Do we seriously suppose that the godless religion of economic determinism which, by its stifling of man's free spirit and its psychiatric prisons for all dissidents, promises mankind a brave new world, after the final show-down between capitalism and communism, will meet man's deepest spiritual need? If you want an answer, read Sol-zhenitzyn's *Gulag Archipelago*.

Or should we pin our hope on humanism with its specious offer of morals without religion? Will this thinly-disguised athe-ism, with its doctrine of man as the thinking reed in an unthink-ing universe, inspire humanity to hope again? Nay, does not history show that in the great scale religion and morals hang together, and that, if you let one go, the other will quickly follow it? How long can men live on a creed which proclaims: 'Be good, although there is no soul of goodness at the heart of things'?

Where, then, should despairing man look today but to that gospel which irradiated long ago that dark pagan world and sustained and inspired our fathers and forefathers in many a cloudy and dark day?

You cannot prove Christianity true as you prove a proposition in Euclid. You can only do so by making the venture of faith and living by it: 'If any man will do his will', Jesus is reported as saying, 'he shall know of the doctrine, whether it be of God' (John 7.17). Yes, but suppose it true. Suppose that the last reality in the universe is not man but a living, loving Father who has revealed his grace and glory in Christ Jesus. Suppose that through the ages 'one increasing purpose runs' which God, the Lord of history, is carrying forward to a blessed conclusion, in spite of all men's sinning. Suppose, further, that, when you have apparently made shipwreck of your life, this gracious God does not give you up but is ready to offer you another chance – forgive you, accept you, and even use you for the furtherance of his high purpose. And suppose, finally, that this divine purpose does not end with death but runs out, beyond this earthly scene, into a better world than this.

This is the hope which lies at the heart of the gospel, and it is founded upon Christ's own triumph over death. 'Only one life has ever won the victory over death,' wrote James Denney, 'and only one life ever can win it: the kind of life which was in Christ, which is in Christ, and which he shares with all whom faith makes one with him. This is our hope, to be really members of

Christ, living with a life which comes from God and has already vanquished death.'[74]

Is not this the hope which mankind needs today if it is to face the future with confidence? It is the confidence that, in spite of all appearances, history is moving to a divinely-appointed end and that, if those who are Christ's, united to him by faith and love, fall asleep before it comes, they but 'sleep to wake', at God's touch, in that eternal world where Christ shall feed his flock like a shepherd and God will wipe away all tears from their eyes.

How should a Christian confront the last enemy when he comes knocking at his door? It is told that when John Knox lay dying, he bade his wife read to him from the Bible, and that when she asked where, he replied. 'Go, read where I first cast my anchor.' So she turned to John's Gospel where down the centuries so many have found comfort and hope in the words of one who spoke of a 'Father's house' with 'many rooms' and promised, 'Because I live, you will live also.' Still later, when Knox could speak no more, someone asked, 'Have you hope?' Knox's answer was simply to turn his eyes upwards to 'the God of hope' who had sustained him all through his stormy life.

Should that not still be the lamp we take for sleeping when we bid the world goodnight?

Notes

1. P. T. Forsyth, *The Church, the Gospel and Society*, Independent Press 1962, p. 84.

2. In *The Interpretation of the Bible*, edited by C. W. Dugmore, SPCK 1944, pp. 92–107.

3. See E. C. Hoskyns and F. N. Davey, *The Riddle of the New Testament*, Faber 1931.

4. P. T. Forsyth, *The Person and Place of Jesus Christ*, Independent Press 1948, p. 122.

5. Rudolf Bultmann, 'Jesus and Paul', in *Existence and Faith. Shorter Writings of Rudolf Bultmann*, edited by Schubert M. Ogden, Fontana Books 1964, pp. 183–201.

6. P. T. Forsyth, *The Person and Place of Jesus Christ*, p. 60.

7. Now chiefly remembered for his hymn 'Amazing Grace' and its haunting melody.

8. For a life of Forsyth and an outline of his theology see my *P. T. Forsyth*, SCM Press 1974.

9. P.T. Forsyth, *Positive Preaching and the Modern Mind*, Hodder and Stoughton 1907. This is perhaps the best all-round summary of Forsyth's theological position. But his greatest book is undoubtedly *The Person and Place of Jesus Christ*.

10. See *The Justification of God*, Independent Press 1957, ch. 12. On the future life generally there are few better books than his *This Life and the Next*, Independent Press 1953.

11. Emil Brunner pronounced Forsyth Britain's greatest modern theologian, and the American Robert Macafee Brown has called him our 'prophet for today'.

12. For this see C. H. Dodd, *The Bible and the Greeks*, Hodder and Stoughton 1935.

13. See John A. T. Robinson, *The Body*, SCM Press 1952.

14. T. R. Glover, *The Conflict of Religions in the Early Roman Empire*, Methuen 1909, p. 155

15. 'Law' here is not to be construed 'legally', for it is incapable of being enforced by external authority.

16. Acts 18.1. Paul worked in Corinth for eighteen months.

17. So C. H. Dodd, *Romans*, Fontana Books 1959, pp. xxxf.

18. It was a politician, the late Richard Crossman, who declared that there was a good deal more evidence in the world today for the Christian dogma of original sin than there was for Marx's doctrine of the classless society.

19. Robert Burns, 'Epistle to Davie'.

20. Some have questioned Paul's authorship. But if it is not by Paul, 'it is a masterly summary of Paul's theology by a disciple who was capable of thinking Paul's thoughts after him' (G. B. Caird).

21. Samuel Taylor Coleridge, in his *Table Talk*.

22. There is probably a reference here to the barrier which separated the inner courts of the Jerusalem Temple from the Court of the Gentiles, a barrier which Gentiles were forbidden to enter on pain of death, Cf. Mark 15.38 with its reference to the rent veil at the crucifixion of Jesus, symbolizing the opening of the way to God by Christ's atoning death.

23. Here we follow tradition and reject G. S. Duncan's view, because we do not certainly know that Paul was ever imprisoned in Ephesus.

24. W. R. Inge, *Outspoken Essays*, Longmans 1919, p. 229.

25. J. D. Michael, *Philippians*, Moffatt New Testament Commentaries, Hodder and Stoughton 1928, p. 201.

26. For Habakkuk, 'faith' meant faithfulness towards God in the convenant relationship and obedience to the commands God had laid on Israel as his chosen people.

27. In this chapter I am much indebted to an article by J. Jeremias, 'Paul and James', *The Expository Times*, September 1955.

28. I have amplified the argument of this chapter in my *According to John*, SCM Press 1968.

29. P. Gardner-Smith, *St John and the Synoptic Gospels*, Cambridge University Press 1938, reopened the whole question.

30. Rudolf Bultmann, *The Theology of the New Testament*, SCM Press 1955, Vol. 2, p. 9.

31. See his essay in the symposium *The Roads Converge*, ed. P. Garner-Smith, Edward Arnold 1963, and his essays in *Twelve New Testament Studies*, SCM Press 1962, pp. 94ff. However, in *Can We Trust the New Testament?*, Mowbrays 1977, he now comes down on the side of apostolic authorship, and dates the gospel just after AD 65.

32. 'John is based on a solid tradition of the works and words of Jesus, a tradition which at times is very primitive. We believe that often John gives us correct historical information about Jesus that no other Gospel has preserved' (Raymond E. Brown, *The Gospel according to John*, Vol. 1, Geoffrey Chapman 1971, p. li).

33. See W. F. Albright's brilliant essay in *The Background of the New Testament and its Eschatology*, edited by W. D. Davies and D. Daube, Cambridge University Press 1954, pp. 153–71.

34. Millar Burrows, *The Dead Sea Scrolls*, Secker and Warburg 1956, p. 340.

35. A. M. Hunter, 'Recent Trends in Johannine Studies', *The Expository Times*, March and April 1960.

36. Those who accept the early martyrdom of John the apostle show a monumental preference for the inferior evidence.

37. For example, the 'Johannine' style of Jesus' *logia*, the improbability that the apostle would have called himself his master's 'favourite pupil', and signs that the gospel has undergone editing (e.g. John 4.2; 21.24), as the Muratorian Canon says it had.

38. F. F. Bruce, *The New Testament Documents*, IVP 1960, p. 53.

39. F. C. Grant pronounced the gospel a work of the second century. His son Robert M. Grant, *A Historical Introduction to the New Testament*, Fontana Books 1971, dates it 'not much later than 70'.

40. B. H. Streeter, in *Oxford Studies in the Synoptic Problem*, ed. W. Sanday, Oxford University Press 1911, pp. 425–36.

41. C. H. Dodd, *The Interpretation of the Fourth Gospel*, Cambridge University Press 1953, p. 447.

42. John A. T. Robinson, in *The Roads Converge*, p. 71.

43. C. K. Barrett, *The Gospel according to St John*, SPCK 1956, p. 362

44. This point is convincingly made by J. E. Davey. The gospel's repeated stress upon Jesus' utter dependence on his heavenly Father (John 5.19; 7.16,28; 8.16; 17.2, etc.) was, he says, never invented by the early church.

45. John A. T. Robinson, *The Roads Converge*, p. 74.

46. T. W. Manson, *On Paul and John*, SCM Press 1963, p. 128.

47. Sir Edwyn Hoskyns, *The Fourth Gospel*, Faber [2]1947, p. 20.

48. Denney used to say that he envied the Roman Catholic priest his crucifix. 'I would like,' he said, 'to go into every church in the land, and, holding up my crucifix, say, "God love like that!" See John Randolph Taylor's splendid study of Denney's theology, *God Loves Like That!*, SCM Press 1962.

49. John Donne, *Eighty Sermons*, London 1640, p. 776.

50. W. R. Inge, *Christian Ethics and Modern Problems*, Hodder 1930, p. 75.

51. Wolfhart Pannenberg, *The Apostles' Creed*, SCM Press 1972, p. 91.

52. T. W. Manson, *The Servant Messiah*, Cambridge University Press 1953, p. 70.

53. Edward Norman, *Christianity and the World Order*, Oxford University Press 1979.

54. *David S. Cairns. An Autobiography*, SCM Press 1950, p. 201.

55. For this whole subject see A. G. Herbert, 'Memory', in *A Theological Word Book of the Bible*, edited by Alan Richardson, SCM Press 1950, pp. 142ff.

56. John V. Taylor, *The Go-Between God*, SCM Press 1972.

57. *David S. Cairns. An Autobiography*, p. 200.

58. Matthew Arnold, 'Obermann once more'.

59. W. J. Hollenweger, *The Pentecostals*, SCM Press 1972, p. 6.

60. Quintin Hogg, *The Door Wherein I Went*, Collins 1975.

61. P. T. Forsyth, *Positive Preaching and the Modern Mind*, p. 3.

62. James S. Stewart, *A Faith to Proclaim*, Hodder and Stoughton 1953, p. 43.

63. Martin Buber, *I and Thee*, T. & T. Clark 1937; [3]1970.

64. Robert Browning, 'Gold Hair', *The Poetical Works of Robert Browning*, Oxford University Press 1905, p. 474.

65. *David S. Cairns. An Autobiography*, p. 37.

66. T. W. Manson, *Ethics and the Gospel*, SCM Press 1960, p. 68.

67. See *The Church Hymnary*, third edition, Hymn 399, for my translation of the hymn's six stanzas.

68. C. L. Mitton, 'Threefoldness in the Teaching of Jesus', *The Expository Times*, May 1964.

69. Robert Browning, 'Saul', *Poetical Works*, p. 228.

70. On this whole subject see D. B. Harned, *Faith and Virtue*, St Andrew Press 1973.

71. For all this see D. S. Cairns, *The Reasonableness of the Christian Faith*, Hodder and Stoughton 1920, chs 1 and 2.

72. A. C. Craig, 'Rooted and Grounded in Love' in *The Sacramental Table* ed. G. J. Jeffrey, James Clarke 1954, p. 50.

73. The traditional rendering of Augustine's *Ama et quod vis, fac*: 'Love, and do as you like' is misleading. It might even be used to justify moral permissiveness unlimited.

74. James Denney, *The Way Everlasting*, Hodder and Stoughton 1911, p. 188.